Table of Contents

Unit	Topic	Page
Unit 1	Vowel short /**a**/, /**e**/	3
Unit 2	Vowel short /**i**/,/**o**/,/**u**/	9
Unit 3	Vowel short /**a**/,/**e**/,/**i**/,/**o**, /**u**/.	15
Unit 4	Vowel short /**e**/	21
Unit 5	Vowels short /**u**/ and /**oo** spelled by **u**/	27
Unit 6	Review tests	209-216
Unit 7	Vowel long /**a**/ /**i**/,/**o**/	34
Unit 8	Vowel long /**a**/	40
Unit 9	Vowel long /**o**/	46
Unit 10	Vowel long /**e**/	52
Unit 11	Vowel long /**i**/	58
Unit 12	Review tests	217-224
Unit 13	**R**-controlled vowel /**or**/ sound	65
Unit 14	**R**-controlled vowel /**er** sound	71
Unit 15	**R**-controlled vowel /**er** sound	77
Unit 16	**R**-controlled vowel /**er**/, /**ar**/	83
Unit 17	Vowel /**o**/	89
Unit 18	Review tests	225-232
Unit 19	Consonant sounds of /**s**/, /**j**/	96
Unit 20	Consonant digraphs **wh**, **ch**, **tch**	102
Unit 21	Consonant clusters **pr**, **dr**	108
Unit 22	Consonant clusters **gl**, **cl**, **bl**.	114
Unit 23	Consonant clusters **mp**, **nd**, **st**; and consonant digraph **ck**	120
Unit 24	Review tests	233-240
Unit 25	Singular possessive**'s**	127
Unit 26	Suffixes **er**, **est**	133
Unit 27	Suffixes **ing**, **ed**	139
Unit 28	Suffix **es**	145
Unit 29	Suffix **ly**	151
Unit 30	Review tests	241-248

Unit 31	Vowel diphthong /**ou**/	158
Unit 32	Vowel /**u**/	164
Unit 33	Compound words	170
Unit 34	Homophones	176
Unit 35	Contractions	182
Unit 36	Review tests	249-256

Spelling glossary..188
Answer Key...257

> It is recommended to remove the answer key and unit tests before book is given to the student. The plans for this book is one page per day Monday through Wednesday. Thursday's work is writing the words two or three times (as directed) on pages provided. The test is to be given on Friday. Review tests are provided for every sixth unit. The recommendation for unit tests is to give one per day.

Cover photo by Ben White
Written by
Victoria Kays

Unit 1

1. camp
2. crash
3. penny
4. clever
5. check
6. apple
7. dragon
8. ranch
9. flash
10. spend
11. bless
12. blend

These words have the short sound of *a* that is heard in *bag* or the short sound of *e* that is heard in *help*.

A. Write the spelling words that have the short **a** sound.

1. _____ 2. _____

3. _____ 4. _____

5. _____ 6. _____

B. Write the spelling words that have the short **e** sound.

1. _____ 2. _____

3. _____ 4. _____

5. _____ 6. _____

C. Write the spelling words that have two syllables.

1. _____ 2. _____

3. _____ 4. _____

D. Write the spelling words that end with a consonant digraph.

1. _____ 2. _____

3. _____

E. Write the spelling word that begins with a consonant digraph.

_____

A. Write the spelling word that goes with each definition.

1. a fruit _____

2. one cent _____

3. to praise _____

4. to break noisily _____

5. a large farm _____

6. smart _____

B. Write these words in alphabetical order.

dragon   camp   flash   spend   blend   check

1. _____

2. _____

3. _____

4. _____

5. _____

6. _____

Write a spelling word in the blank to finish the sentence.

1. A Komodo _____ is a big lizard.

2. Mr. Johnson lived on a _____ in Texas.

3. Did they _____ outside all night?

4. _____ the cookie mix with an egg and oil.

5. A _____ is a copper color coin.

6. James is a very _____ man to learn so quickly.

7. We heard the _____ of the tree.

8. Please _____ to see if the light is off in the room.

9. We should not _____ too much money on silly things.

10. Some people might say, "_____ you," if they think you are hurting.

11. Did you see a _____ of lightning?

12. I wanted to get an _____ instead of an orange.

6

Write the spelling words three times each.

1. camp _____ _____

   _____

2. crash _____ _____

   _____

3. penny _____ _____

   _____

4. clever _____

   _____

   _____

5. check _____ _____

   _____

6. apple _____ _____

   _____

7. dragon _____

_____

_____

8. ranch _____

_____

_____

9. flash _____ _____

_____

10. spend _____ _____

_____

11. bless _____ _____

_____

12. blend _____ _____

_____

Unit 2

1. shock
2. still
3. cluster
4. rock
5. pond
6. grill
7. flush
8. splint
9. crush
10. glob
11. glimmer
12. brunch

These words have the short sound of *o* that is heard in ***hot***, the short sound of *i* that is heard in ***hit***, or the short sound of *u* that is heard in ***drum***.

A. Write the spelling words that have the short **o** sound.

1. _____ 2. _____

3. _____ 4. _____

B. Write the spelling words that have the short **i** sound.

1. _____ 2. _____

3. _____ 4. _____

C. Write the spelling words that have the short **u** sound.

1. _____ 2. _____

3. _____ 4. _____

D. Write the spelling words that have two syllables.

1. _____ 2. _____

E. Write the spelling words that have double consonants.

1. _____ 2. _____

3. _____

F. Write the spelling words that end with a consonant digraph.

1. _____ 2. _____

3. _____

A. Write a spelling word that rhymes with each word.

1. rock _____

2. fond _____

3. rob _____

4. lunch _____

5. still _____

6. rent _____

B. Write these words in alphabetical order.

cluster   flush   crush   rock   glimmer   still

1. _____

2. _____

3. _____

4. _____

5. _____

6. _____

Write a spelling word in each blank to finish the sentences.

1. We can cook hamburgers on a _____.

2. We can eat _____ at 11:00 A.M. then go fishing.

3. Do not throw a _____ in the _____.

4. Two men came back with a huge _____ of grapes.

5. If you _____ your leg, we can put a _____ on it until you can go to a doctor.

6. Spray water in the pipe to _____ junk out of it.

7. You might feel a _____ if you touch an electrical wire.

8. The _____ from the sun was bright.

9. Be sure to not get a _____ of mud on your clothes.

10. Be _____ and watch the pond for fish.

Write the spelling words three times each.

1. shock _____ _____

   _____

2. still _____ _____

   _____

3. cluster _____

   _____

   _____

4. rock _____ _____

   _____

5. pond _____ _____

   _____

6. grill _____ _____

   _____

7. flush _____ _____

   _____

8. splint _____

_____

_____

9. crush _____ _____

_____

10. glob _____ _____

_____

11. glimmer _____

_____

_____

12. brunch _____

_____

_____

Unit 3

1. land
2. sang
3. began
4. when
5. fence
6. drink
7. twin
8. silver
9. drop
10. dollar
11. truck
12. until

The words in this unit have short vowel sounds.

A. Write a spelling word that rhymes with each word.

1. band _____   2. bang _____

3. top _____   4. duck _____

B. Write the spelling words that have the **short i** sound.

1. _____   2. _____

3. _____   4. _____

C. Write the spelling words that have the **short e** sound.

1. _____   2. _____

D. Write the spelling words that have the **short u** sound.

1. _____   2. _____

E. Write the spelling words that have two syllables.

1. _____   2. _____

3. _____   4. _____

Write the spelling word that goes with each definition.

1. a wall with a gate _____

2. at what time _____

3. a shiny metal _____

4. a small bit of liquid _____

5. one hundred pennies _____

6. the ground _____

7. did sing _____

8. a vehicle in which you can carry things

   _____

9. someone who was born to the same parents at the same time as

   someone else _____

10. to start _____

11. to swallow a liquid _____

12. up to that time _____

Write a spelling word to complete each sentence.

1. The men _____ working on the road.

2. This _____ is called the U. S. A.

3. She _____ the song "Wonderful Peace."

4. The water was running over the top of the _____ during the flood.

5. You can work _____ the alarm sounds.

6. Please get me a _____ of water.

7. James has been driving a four-wheel drive _____.

8. Do you have a _____ coin?

9. _____ we get tired, we should rest.

10. Stephanie was Ricky's _____ sister.

11. Do not _____ the glass jar.

12. The ribbon costs one _____.

Write the spelling words three times each.

1. land _____ _____

   _____

2. sang _____ _____

   _____

3. began _____ _____

   _____

4. when _____ _____

   _____

5. fence _____ _____

   _____

6. drink _____ _____

   _____

7. twin _____ _____

   _____

8. silver _____ _____

   _____

9. drop _____ _____

   _____

10. dollar _____ _____

    _____

11. truck _____ _____

    _____

12. until _____ _____

    _____

Unit 4

1. head
2. read
3. already
4. ready
5. ahead
6. lead
7. breakfast
8. thread
9. heavy
10. instead
11. breath
12. weather

These words have the short sound of *e* spelled by the letters *ea*.

A. Write spelling words that rhyme with **spread**.

1. _____ 2. _____

3. _____ 4. _____

5. _____ 6. _____

B. Write the spelling words that have two syllables.

1. _____ 2. _____

3. _____ 4. _____

5. _____ 6. _____

C. Write the spelling word that has three syllables.

_____

D. Write the spelling words that end in **y**.

1. _____ 2. _____

3. _____

E. Make new words by joining these words and word endings.

1. head + ed _____

2. head + ing _____

Use the code to find the spelling words.

1	2	3	4	5	6	7	8	9	10
a	b	d	e	f	h	i	k	l	n
11	12	13	14	15	16				
r	s	t	v	w	y				

1. 1 + 9 + 11 + 4 + 1 + 3 + 16 _____

2. 15 + 4 + 1 + 13 + 6 + 4 + 11 _____

3. 2 + 11 + 4 + 1 + 13 + 6 _____

4. 2 + 11 + 4 + 1 + 8 + 5 + 1 + 12 + 13

   _____

5. 6 + 4 + 1 + 14 + 16 _____

6. 13 + 6 + 11 + 4 + 1 + 3 _____

7. 11 + 4 + 1 + 3 + 16 _____

8. 7 + 10 + 12 + 13 + 4 + 1 + 3 _____

9. 1 + 6 + 4 + 1 + 3 _____

10. 9 + 4 + 1 + 3 _____

11. 11 + 4 + 1 + 3 _____

12. 6 + 4 + 1 + 3 _____

Write a spelling word to complete each sentence.

1. Darien wanted Vickie to cook a big _____ for the students.

2. She was _____ cooking when they came into the school.

3. Some students would eat _____ of doing school work.

4. The food was finally _____ to eat.

5. Vickie wanted them to go _____ and eat.

6. The boy that was _____ would eat the most.

7. Who _____ them in prayer before the meal?

8. The _____ was cool outside.

9. You should have your _____ covered to keep from catching a cold.

10. She _____ the story to them.

11. You can sew _____.

12. Don't run too fast! Take time to catch your _____.

Write the spelling words three times each.

1. head _____ _____

   _____

2. read _____ _____

   _____

3. already_____

   _____

   _____

4. ready _____ _____

   _____

5. ahead _____ _____

   _____

6. lead _____ _____

   _____

7. breakfast _____

_____

_____

8. thread _____   _____

_____

9. heavy _____   _____

_____

10. instead _____   _____

_____

11. breath _____   _____

_____

12. weather _____

_____

_____

Unit 5

1. good
2. stood
3. wooden
4. hum
5. pull
6. under
7. uncle
8. butter
9. bush
10. supper
11. husband
12. could

These words have the vowel sound heard in *full* or *pup*. The *u* sound can be spelled by the letters *oo*, *u*, or *ou*.

A. Write the spelling words that have the vowel sound you hear in **full**.

1. _____ 2. _____

3. _____ 4. _____

5. _____ 6. _____

B. Write the spelling words that have the vowel sound you hear in **cup**.

1. _____ 2. _____

3. _____ 4. _____

5. _____ 6. _____

C. Write the spelling words that have two syllables.

1. _____ 2. _____

3. _____ 4. _____

5. _____ 6. _____

A. Write these spelling words in alphabetical order.

    stood   hum   bush   could   pull   good

1. _____   2. _____

3. _____   4. _____

5. _____   6. _____

B. Divide these words into syllables. Put a hyphen between the syllables. Use your spelling glossary.

    wooden   under   uncle   butter   supper   husband

1. _____   2. _____

3. _____   4. _____

5. _____   6. _____

C. One word in each group is misspelled. Write it correctly.

    1. under   could   unkle _____

    2. supur   butter   wooden _____

    3. good   bush   stod _____

    4. hisband   hum   pull _____

Write the spelling word that goes with each meaning.

1. a man that is married _____

2. nice _____

3. the husband of your aunt _____

4. the evening meal _____

5. to sing with the lips closed _____

6. made of logs or boards _____

7. a dairy product used on food to make it have a better taste

   _____

8. below _____

9. was able to _____

10. to draw something toward you _____

11. did stand _____

12. a small tree or shrub _____

Write the spelling words three times each.

1. good _____ _____

   _____

2. stood _____ _____

   _____

3. wooden _____ _____

   _____

4. hum _____ _____

   _____

5. pull _____ _____

   _____

6. under _____ _____

   _____

7. uncle _____   _____

   _____

8. butter _____   _____

   _____

9. bush _____   _____

   _____

10. supper _____   _____

    _____

11. husband _____

    _____

    _____

12. could _____   _____

    _____

Unit 6
Review

Ask teacher for test.

Part 1 Grade _____

Part 2 Grade _____

Part 3 Grade _____

Part 4 Grade _____

Unit 7

1. shave
2. state
3. wise
4. stole
5. close
6. glide
7. plate
8. broke
9. white
10. flame
11. stove
12. smile

These spelling words have the long vowel sounds of *a*, *i*, and *o* spelled by the **vowel** + **consonant** + *e* pattern.

shave   state   wise   stole   close   glide
plate   broke   white   flame   stove   smile

A. Write the spelling words that have the long **a** sound.

1. _____   2. _____

3. _____   4. _____

B. Write the spelling words that have the long **i** sound.

1. _____   2. _____

3. _____   4. _____

C. Write the spelling words that have the long **o** sound.

1. _____   2. _____

3. _____   4. _____

D. Write the spelling words that begin with the consonant cluster **st**.

1. _____   2. _____

3. _____

E. Write the spelling words that begin with a consonant digraph.

1. _____   2. _____

A. Write the spelling word for each dictionary respelling.

1. (shāv) _____

2. (wīz) _____

3. (plāt) _____

4. (brōk) _____

5. (flām) _____

6. (wīt) _____

7. (stōv) _____

8. (stōl) _____

B. Write these words in a-b-c order.

    state   close   glide   smile

1. _____

2. _____

3. _____

4. _____

C. Write the spelling word that is the opposite of these words.

1. frown _____

2. open _____

Write a spelling word in the blank to finish the sentence.

1. The little boy was sad after he _____ the toy airplane.

2. Is the weather in your _____ always cold?

3. There was a _____ on the baby's face.

4. The bride wore a _____ dress.

5. Solomon was a _____ king.

6. We can cook beans on the _____.

7. It was fun to _____ down the long slide.

8. Do not touch the hot _____ on the stove.

9. The man went to jail because he _____ the trailer.

10. James likes to _____ his beard after he takes a shower.

11. Please _____ the door.

12. I like to put my food on a blue _____.

Write the spelling words three times each.

1. shave _____ _____

   _____

2. state _____ _____

   _____

3. wise _____ _____

   _____

4. stole _____ _____

   _____

5. close _____ _____

   _____

6. glide _____ _____

   _____

7. plate _____ _____

_____

8. broke _____ _____

_____

9. white _____ _____

_____

10. flame _____ _____

_____

11. stove _____ _____

_____

12. smile _____ _____

_____

Unit 8

1. rain   2. paid

3. wait   4. afraid

5. paint   6. plain

7. stay   8. today

9. away   10. maybe

11. hay   12. tray

These words have the **long** *a* sound spelled by the letters *ai* or *ay*.

rain paid wait afraid paint plain
stay today away maybe hay tray

A. Write the spelling words in which the long **a** sound is spelled **ai**.

1. _____ 2. _____

3. _____ 4. _____

5. _____ 6. _____

B. Write the spelling words in which the long **a** sound is spelled **ay**.

1. _____ 2. _____

3. _____ 4. _____

5. _____ 6. _____

C. Write the spelling words that have two syllables.

1. _____ 2. _____

3. _____ 4. _____

D. Write these compound words.

1. may + be _____

2. to + day _____

A. Write the spelling word that goes with each meaning.

1. possible; perhaps _____

2. scared _____

3. drops of falling water _____

4. gave money away for something _____

5. to stay _____

6. this day _____

B. Write these words in alphabetical order.

paint   plain   stay   away   hay   tray

1. _____ 2. _____

3. _____ 4. _____

5. _____ 6. _____

C. A word in each sentence is misspelled. Write the words correctly.

1. Do you think it will rane today? _____

2. Some dogs are afrayed of thunder. _____

3. Maibe the clouds will go away. _____

Write the spelling word that belongs in each sentence.

1. Will you _____ this room for me?

2. Who _____ for the train ride?

3. My aunt went _____ for a long time.

4. I hope it does not _____ today.

5. Horses eat _____.

6. Please hold your _____ with both hands.

7. I am _____ of big dogs.

8. Will you please _____ for me?

9. The dress was _____, not fancy.

10. I would like to get out of school early _____.

11. _____ everyone will get finished early.

12. If we don't get finished, we will _____ until it's time to go home.

Write the spelling words three times each.

1. rain _____ _____

   _____

2. paid _____ _____

   _____

3. wait _____ _____

   _____

4. afraid _____ _____

   _____

5. paint _____ _____

   _____

6. plain _____ _____

   _____

7. stay _____ _____

_____

8. today _____ _____

_____

9. away _____ _____

_____

10. maybe _____ _____

_____

11. hay _____ _____

_____

12. tray _____ _____

_____

Unit 9

1. road
2. coat
3. load
4. boat
5. hold
6. fold
7. ago
8. over
9. open
10. only
11. toe
12. hello

These words have the **long *o*** sound spelled by the letters *o*, *oa*, or *oe*.

road   coat   load   boat   hold   fold
ago   over   open   only   toe   hello

A. Write the spelling words in which the long **o** sound is spelled **oa**.

1. _____ 2. _____

3. _____ 4. _____

B. Write the spelling words that contain the word **old**.

1. _____ 2. _____

C. Write the spelling words that have two syllables.

1. _____ 2. _____

3. _____ 4. _____

5. _____

D. Write the word that has double consonants.

_____

E. Write the spelling word that has the long **o** sound spelled by the letters **oe**.

_____

47

A. There are two words at the top of every page of your spelling glossary. These words are called **guide words**.
The guide word at the top left is the first entry word on that page. The guide word at the top right is the last entry word on that page. Look at these guide words. Write the spelling word or words that would be on the same page as the guide words.

1. **fog - foot** _____

2. **only – owe** _____ _____

   _____

3. **agree – boot** _____

4. **thread – twin** _____

B. Write these words in alphabetical order.

    road   coat   load   boat   hold   hello

1. _____ 2. _____

3. _____ 4. _____

5. _____ 6. _____

A. Write the spelling word that goes with each meaning.

1. to grasp and keep _____
2. gone by, past _____
3. a small ship _____
4. above _____
5. by itself _____
6. not shut _____
7. a street _____
8. a greeting _____
9. a crease or wrinkle _____
10. a piece of clothing to keep you warm _____
11. a part of the foot _____
12. something to be carried _____

B. Write the words that complete the puzzle.

1. hold - h + f = _____
2. boat - b + c = _____

Write the spelling words three times each.

1. road _____ _____

   _____

2. coat _____ _____

   _____

3. load _____ _____

   _____

4. boat _____ _____

   _____

5. hold _____ _____

   _____

6. fold _____ _____

   _____

7. ago _____ _____

_____

8. over _____ _____

_____

9. open _____ _____

_____

10. only _____ _____

_____

11. toe _____ _____

_____

12. hello _____ _____

_____

Unit 10

1. seat 2. clean

3. read 4. mean

5. leap 6. peep

7. feel 8. asleep

9. street 10. peek

11. keep 12. needle

These spelling words have the **long** *e* sound spelled by the letters *ea* or *ee*.

seat   clean   read   mean   leap   peep
feel   asleep   street   peek   keep   needle

A. Write the spelling words in which the long **e** sound is spelled **ea**.

1. _____   2. _____

3. _____   4. _____

5. _____

B. Write the spelling words in which the long **e** sound is spelled **ee**.

1. _____   2. _____

3. _____   4. _____

5. _____   6. _____

7. _____

C. Write the spelling words that have two syllables.

1. _____   2. _____

D. Write the word that completes each rhyme.

1. It isn't fair to _____ if a surprise you seek.

2. How might a fish _____ to be caught with rod and reel?

A. Take **ed** away from these words to make spelling words. Write the words.

1. cleaned _____

2. peeped _____

3. seated _____

4. leaped _____

B. Write these words in alphabetical order.

read   asleep   mean   street   feel   peek

1. _____ 2. _____

3. _____ 4. _____

5. _____ 6. _____

C. Write the spelling word that means the opposite of each word.

1. dirty _____

2. nice _____

3. awake _____

4. to give away _____

Write the spelling word that belongs in each sentence.

1. You can use a _____ and thread to sew the dress.

2. Please _____ this money for me.

3. Were you _____ when I called?

4. Sit down in the brown _____.

5. A little chicken sounds like it says _____.

6. The clothes were _____.

7. What is the name of your _____?

8. It is not fair to _____ when you play hide and seek.

9. James likes to _____ about dinosaurs.

10. Do you _____ well today?

11. I do not like to be a _____ teacher.

12. They like to _____ into the pile of leaves.

Write the spelling words three times each.

1. seat _____ _____

   _____

2. clean_____ _____

   _____

3. read _____ _____

   _____

4. mean _____ _____

   _____

5. leap _____ _____

   _____

6. peep _____ _____

   _____

7. feel _____   _____

_____

8. asleep _____   _____

_____

9. street _____   _____

_____

10. peek _____   _____

_____

11. keep _____   _____

_____

12. needle _____

_____

_____

Unit 11

1. high
2. light

3. night
4. right

5. bright
6. my

7. cry
8. dry

9. tie
10. lie

11. sky
12. fly

These spelling words have the **long *i*** sound spelled by the letters *igh*, *y*, or *ie*.

high light night right bright my
cry dry tie lie sky fly

A. Write the spelling words in which the long **i** sound is spelled **y**.

1. _____ 2. _____

3. _____ 4. _____

5. _____

B. Write the spelling words in which the long **i** sound is spelled **igh**.

1. _____ 2. _____

3. _____ 4. _____

5. _____

C. Write the spelling words that have the same ending as **die**.

1. _____ 2. _____

D. Write the word that completes each rhyme.

1. The kite flew _____ in the sky.

2. Turn on the _____ when it gets

to be night.

A. Write the spelling word that means the opposite of each word.

1. low _____ 2. dark _____

3. left _____ 4. wet _____

5. day _____ 6. laugh _____

7. earth _____ 8. untie _____

B. Write the spelling word for each dictionary respelling.

1. (brīt) _____

2. (lī) _____

3. (mī) _____

4. (flī) _____

C. Write sentences using these words.

    light   **bright**   **right**

1. _____

_____

2. _____

_____

3. _____

_____

Write the spelling word that belongs in each sentence.

1. It is fun to _____ a kite on a windy day.

2. You have to be careful, or your kite might not go very _____.

3. You want your kite to fly high in the _____.

4. It is important to _____ the string on the kite in the _____ place.

5. Do not try to fly your kite at _____.

6. You will not want to look at the _____ sun.

7. You should keep your kite in a _____ place when you're not flying it.

8. Do not _____ if your kite doesn't go up the first time.

9. Do not let it _____ on the ground and get wet.

10. A _____ blue or dark kite would be pretty.

11. _____ kite could be the best.

Write the spelling words three times each.

1. high _____ _____

   _____

2. light _____ _____

   _____

3. night _____ _____

   _____

4. right _____ _____

   _____

5. bright _____ _____

   _____

6. my _____ _____

   _____

7. cry _____ _____

_____

8. dry _____ _____

_____

9. tie _____ _____

_____

10. lie _____ _____

_____

11. sky _____ _____

_____

12. fly _____ _____

_____

Unit 12
Review

Ask teacher for test.

Part 1 Grade _____

Part 2 Grade _____

Part 3 Grade _____

Part 4 Grade _____

Unit 13

1. pour
2. short
3. born
4. horse
5. fork
6. north
7. store
8. more
9. score
10. story
11. roar
12. board

These spelling words have an *r*-controlled *o* spelled by the letters *or*, *our*, *oar*, or *ore*.

pour short born horse fork north
store more score story roar board

A. Write the spelling words in which the **or** sound is spelled by the letters **or**.

1. _____ 2. _____

3. _____ 4. _____

5. _____ 6. _____

B. Write the spelling words in which the **or** sound is spelled by the letters **ore**.

1. _____ 2. _____

3. _____

C. Write the spelling words in which the **or** sound is spelled by the letters **oar**.

1. _____ 2. _____

D. Write the spelling word in which the **or** sound is spelled by the letters **our**.

_____

A. Read the spelling words listed below. Write the letter of its dictionary respelling beside each word.

1. pour _____   A. (skôr)

2. story _____   B. (shôrt)

3. score _____   C. (bôrd)

4. short _____   D. (rôr)

5. roar _____   E. (stôr′ ē)

6. board _____   F. (pôr)

B. Write the spelling word that is the opposite of each word.

1. less _____ 2. tall _____

3. south _____ 4. die _____

C. Write the word that goes with each meaning.

1. a place where goods are sold _____

2. an eating tool _____

3. a work animal _____

Write the spelling word that belongs in each sentence.

1. The _____ of a lion is loud.

2. What was the _____ when University of Kentucky won the game?

3. Would you please _____ me some milk?

4. Ohio is _____ of Tennessee.

5. A _____ is an animal that many people like to ride.

6. I would like some _____ candy.

7. I went to the _____ to buy some candy.

8. On what date were you _____?

9. The wooden _____ helped make the step sturdy.

10. Some students thought the woman was young because she was _____.

11. I told the children the _____ of Joseph.

12. Please use your _____ to eat the corn.

Write the spelling words three times each.

1. pour _____ _____

   _____

2. short _____ _____

   _____

3. born _____ _____

   _____

4. horse _____ _____

   _____

5. fork _____ _____

   _____

6. north _____ _____

   _____

7. store _____ _____

   _____

8. more _____ _____

   _____

9. score _____ _____

   _____

10. story _____ _____

    _____

11. roar _____ _____

    _____

12. board _____

    _____

    _____

Unit 14

1. worm
2. work
3. word
4. worth
5. worry
6. earn
7. early
8. earth
9. learn
10. heard
11. person
12. were

These spelling words have the *er* sound heard in *term* spelled by the letters *or*, *er*, or *ear*.

worm   work   word   worth   worry   earn
early   earth   learn   heard   person   were

A. Write the spelling words in which the vowel **o** is controlled by the consonant **r** and has the **er** sound.

1. _____   2. _____

3. _____   4. _____

5. _____

B. Write the spelling words in which vowel **e** is controlled by the consonant **r** and has the **er** sound.

1. _____   2. _____

C. Write the spelling words in which the **er** sound is spelled by the letters **ear**.

1. _____   2. _____

3. _____   4. _____

5. _____

D. Write the spelling words that have two syllables.

1. _____   2. _____

3. _____

A. Write the spelling word for each dictionary respelling.

1. (wėrk) _____ 2. (ėrth) _____

3. (wėrd) _____ 4. (hėrd) _____

5. (wėr) _____ 6. (lėrn) _____

7. (ėrn) _____ 8. (wėrth) _____

9. (wėrm) _____ 10. (wėr′ ē) _____

B. One of the words is misspelled in each row. Write the word correctly.

1. wurm   work   worry   _____

2. person   earth   weer   _____

3. learrn   worth   early   _____

4. heard   woord   earn   _____

5. word   person   earht   _____

6. learn   worre   heard   _____

C. Write the word that goes with each meaning.

1. a small legless animal used for fishing _____

2. the planet where we live _____

Write the spelling word that belongs in each sentence.

1. The man does the _____ with a big machine.

2. The big _____ could be used for fishing.

3. We can _____ a lot if we read the right kind of books.

4. More than one _____ is called people.

5. We get up _____ almost every morning.

6. You put letters together to make a _____.

7. We _____ going out to eat for breakfast.

8. Please do not _____ about me.

9. I _____ that big noise.

10. How much is the car _____?

11. The _____ is the third planet from the sun.

12. You can _____ some money if you will work.

Write the spelling words three times each.

1. worm _____ _____

   _____

2. work _____ _____

   _____

3. word _____ _____

   _____

4. worth _____ _____

   _____

5. worry _____ _____

   _____

6. earn _____ _____

   _____

7. early _____   _____

_____

8. earth _____   _____

_____

9. learn _____   _____

_____

10. heard _____   _____

_____

11. person _____

_____

_____

12. were _____   _____

_____

Unit 15

1. bird
2. shirt
3. first
4. third
5. sir
6. birthday
7. turn
8. burn
9. hurt
10. church
11. turtle
12. hurry

These spelling words have the *er* sound heard in *term* spelled by the letters *ur* and *ir*.

bird   shirt   first   third   sir   birthday
turn   burn   hurt   church   turtle   hurry

A. Write the spelling words in which **er** sound is spelled by the letters **ir**.

1. _____   2. _____

3. _____   4. _____

5. _____   6. _____

B. Write the spelling words in which **er** sound is spelled by the letters **ur**.

1. _____   2. _____

3. _____   4. _____

5. _____   6. _____

C. Write the spelling words that have two syllables.

1. _____   2. _____

3. _____

D. Write the spelling words that name animals.

1. _____   2. _____

A. Write the spelling word for each dictionary respelling.

1. (bėrd) _____ 2. (shėrt) _____

3. (fėrst) _____ 4. (sėr) _____

5. (thėrd) _____ 6. (hėrt) _____

7. (bėrn) _____ 8. (tėrn) _____

9. (hėr′ ē) _____

10. (chėrch) _____

B. Write the spelling words that would be on the same page as the guide words.

1. **fire - for** _____

2. **better - bite** _____ _____

3. **tie - twin** _____ _____

4. **hole - husband** _____ _____

5. **shut - smile** _____ _____

6. **tell - tie** _____

7. **chance - climb** _____

8. **boat - certain** _____

Write the spelling word that belongs in each sentence.

1. The _____ thing you should do in the mornings is to pray.

2. Please _____ up the heat.

3. He started a fire to _____ the trash.

4. You should go to _____ every Sunday.

5. My mother used to have a yellow _____ that sang in its cage.

6. You should say _____ when you are talking to a man.

7. Please _____ and eat your breakfast.

8. He was wearing a white _____ in the wedding.

9. November 3 is the _____ day of the month.

10. November 2 is Richard's _____.

11. Vickie _____ her leg when she fell.

12. A _____ walks very slowly.

Write the spelling words three times each.

1. bird _____ _____

   _____

2. shirt _____ _____

   _____

3. first _____ _____

   _____

4. third _____ _____

   _____

5. sir _____ _____

   _____

6. birthday _____

   _____

   _____

7. turn _____   _____

_____

8. burn _____   _____

_____

9. hurt _____   _____

_____

10. church _____   _____

_____

11. turtle _____

_____

_____

12. hurry _____   _____

_____

Unit 16

1. air
2. fair
3. stairs
4. there
5. pair
6. chair
7. care
8. stare
9. wear
10. bear
11. where
12. their

These spelling words have the *r*-controlled *a* heard in *care* spelled *air*, *are*, *ear*, *eir* or *ere*.

air   fair   stairs   there   pair   chair
care   stare   wear   bear   where   their

A. Write the spelling words that have the vowels **ai** controlled by the consonant **r**.

1. _____   2. _____

3. _____   4. _____

5. _____

B. Write the spelling words that have the **r**-controlled vowel sound heard in **care** spelled by the letters **are**.

1. _____   2. _____

C. Words that sound alike but have different spellings and meanings are called **homophones**. Write the spelling word that is a homophone for **their**.

_____

D. Write the spelling words that begin with the letter **w**.

1. _____   2. _____

A. Write the spelling word that is a homophone for each of these words. You will need to add **s** to one word.

1. fare _____ 2. stairs _____

3. their _____ 4. pear _____

5. bare _____

B. Write the spelling words that would be on the same dictionary page as these guide words.

1. **weak - weave** _____

2. **thee - they** _____ _____

3. **stain - stark** _____ _____

4. **car - careless** _____

5. **what - who** _____

6. **aid - alarm** _____

7. **chain - climb** _____

8. **bat - certain** _____

A. Add a word to each spelling word to make a compound word.

1. air + line _____

2. care + less _____

3. any + where _____

4. up + stairs _____

B. Write the spelling word that fits both sentences in each set.

1. We breathe _____.

   Planes fly in the _____.

2. I have a purple coat to _____.

   Writing will _____ down your pencil.

C. Write the spelling word that belongs in each sentence.

1. I got a new _____ of tennis shoes.

2. There were many booths at the Fairdale _____.

3. Did you go _____?

4. We took a blue _____ to sit in.

5. I would be afraid if a polar _____ were to

   _____ at me for a very long time.

Write the spelling words three times each.

1. air _____ _____

   _____

2. fair _____ _____

   _____

3. stairs _____ _____

   _____

4. there _____ _____

   _____

5. pair _____ _____

   _____

6. chair _____ _____

   _____

7. care _____   _____

   _____

8. stare _____   _____

   _____

9. wear _____   _____

   _____

10. bear _____   _____

    _____

11. where _____   _____

    _____

12. their _____   _____

    _____

Unit 17

1. raw 2. jaw

3. straw 4. thaw

5. saw 6. draw

7. slaw 8. law

9. lawn 10. yawn

11. fawn 12. hawk

The words in this unit have an *a* that is controlled by the letter *w*.

raw   jaw   straw   thaw   saw   draw
slaw   law   lawn   yawn   fawn   hawk

A. Write the spelling words in which the vowel sound you hear in **saw** is at the end of the word.

1. _____ 2. _____

3. _____ 4. _____

5. _____ 6. _____

7. _____ 8. _____

B. Write the spelling words in which the **w-controlled a** sound is in the middle of the word.

1. _____ 2. _____

3. _____ 4. _____

C. Write the spelling word that names a part of the body.

_____

D. Write the spelling words that name animals.

1. _____ 2. _____

A. Write a spelling word for each dictionary respelling.

1. (jô) _____ 2. (sô) _____

3. (drô) _____ 4. (slô) _____

5. (yôn) _____ 6. (strô) _____

B. Write a spelling word for each meaning.

1. not cooked _____

2. a rule to live by _____

3. to melt _____

4. green grass in your yard _____

5. a baby deer _____

6. a large bird _____

C. Write the spelling word that completes both sentences.

1. We _____ the deer beside the road.

2. The man used a _____ to cut the wood.

Write a spelling word to complete each sentence. You will need to add **s** to one word.

1. I got a _____ to put into my cup.

2. When people are tired, they may _____.

3. I like cabbage as long as it is _____.

4. A _____ is a very large bird.

5. We should lay the turkey out to let it _____.

6. An attorney should know the _____ of our state.

7. A baby deer is called a _____.

8. Put chopped cabbage carrots together to make _____.

9. Will you _____ a picture for me?

10. The lower _____ bone is called the mandible.

11. I mowed the _____ with a riding mower.

12. We _____ many deer beside that road at night.

Write the spelling words three times each.

1. raw _____ _____

   _____

2. jaw _____ _____

   _____

3. straw _____ _____

   _____

4. thaw _____ _____

   _____

5. saw _____ _____

   _____

6. draw _____ _____

   _____

7. slaw _____ _____

   _____

8. law _____ _____

   _____

9. lawn _____ _____

   _____

10. yawn _____ _____

    _____

11. fawn _____ _____

    _____

12. hawk _____ _____

    _____

Unit 18
Review

Ask teacher for test.

Part 1 Grade _____

Part 2 Grade _____

Part 3 Grade _____

Part 4 Grade _____

Unit 19

1. cent
2. circle
3. certain
4. circus
5. chance
6. city
7. giant
8. cage
9. large
10. orange
11. change
12. danger

The words in this unit have the "soft" sound of *c* or *g*. When a *c* is followed by an *e*, *i*, or *y*, it has the soft sound which is like the sound of an *s*. When a *g* is followed by an *e*, *i*, or *y*, it usually has the soft sound which is the sound of a *j*.

cent   circle   certain   circus   chance   city

giant   cage   large   orange   change   danger

A. Write the spelling words that have the soft sound of **c**.

1. _____   2. _____

3. _____   4. _____

5. _____   6. _____

B. Write the spelling words that have the soft sound of **g**.

1. _____   2. _____

3. _____   4. _____

5. _____   6. _____

C. Write the spelling word that is a homophone for **sent**.

_____

D. Write the spelling word that rhymes with each of these words.

1. range _____   2. tent _____

3. barge _____   4. dance _____

A. Write these words in syllables. Put hyphens between the syllables. Use your spelling dictionary.

1. circle _____

2. certain _____

3. circus _____

4. giant _____

5. orange _____

6. danger _____

7. city _____

B. Write a spelling word for each dictionary respelling.

1. (sėr′ kəl) _____

2. (chăns) _____

3. (chānj) _____

4. (kāj) _____

5. (lärj) _____

6. (sĭnt) _____

C. One word is misspelled in each row. Write it correctly.

1. circle   sertain   chance _____

2. orang   large   cage _____

Write a spelling word to complete each sentence. You will need to add **s** to one word.

1. One day I went to the _____.

2. It seemed the tiger trainer was in _____ of being eaten by a tiger.

3. The tigers were _____ and black.

4. They were in a _____ cage.

5. I did not want to be in the _____ with them.

6. I was not _____ that they would not get out.

7. This circus was in the _____ of Louisville.

8. It did not cost me one _____, but I do not want another _____ to go because I did not like it.

9. I do not think anything will _____ my mind.

10. I would rather have seen a big tall _____ than to watch the people who were walking a tight rope.

11. I would rather sit and draw _____ than to go back to see those scary sights.

Write the spelling words three times each.

1. cent _____   _____

   _____

2. circle _____   _____

   _____

3. certain_____   _____

   _____

4. circus _____   _____

   _____

5. chance_____   _____

   _____

6. city   _____   _____

   _____

7. giant _____ _____

_____

8. cage _____ _____

_____

9. large _____ _____

_____

10. orange _____ _____

_____

11. change _____ _____

_____

12. danger _____

_____

_____

Unit 20

1. wheel
2. while
3. chin
4. chase
5. why
6. whisper
7. branch
8. teach
9. inch
10. watch
11. catch
12. child

A set of letters that spells one sound is called a **digraph**. These words have the *ch*, *tch*, or *wh* digraph.

wheel   while   chin   chase   why   whisper

branch   teach   inch   watch   catch   child

A. Write the spelling words that begin with the consonant digraph **ch**.

1. _____   2. _____

3. _____

B. Write the spelling words that have the **ch** sound spelled **tch**.

1. _____   2. _____

C. Write the spelling words that end with the consonant digraph **ch**.

1. _____   2. _____

3. _____

D. Write the spelling words that begin with the consonant cluster **wh**.

1. _____   2. _____

3. _____   4. _____

A. Pretend the dictionary is divided into three parts.

Part 1	**Part 2**	**Part 3**
Letters A-D	Letters E-L	Letters M-Z

Beside each word write **1**, **2**, or **3** to show in which part of the dictionary you would look to find the word.

1. teach _____   2. chin _____   3. inch _____

4. wheel _____ 5. branch _____ 6. catch _____

B. Write the spelling word that goes with each meaning.

1. the part of your face below your mouth _____

2. a small clock worn on the wrist _____

3. to help someone learn _____

4. to get hold of something _____

5. the round part of a car that touches the ground

   _____

6. the part of a tree that has leaves _____

7. one of twelve parts of a foot ruler _____

8. to run after _____

9. to talk in a low voice _____

Write a spelling word to complete each sentence.

1. Enjoy the weather _____ it is warm.

2. Wear warm clothes when it is cold, so you won't _____ a cold.

3. Learn all you can, so you can _____ others.

4. You should talk in a _____ voice in the library.

5. You can _____ others around if you are "it" in the game of frozen catchers.

6. The _____ band was almost broken.

7. Thirteen inches is one more _____ than a foot.

8. The _____ on the trailer was flat.

9. I am ticklish under my _____.

10. The tree _____ was low enough for Donna to step onto it and climb up the tree.

11. The small _____ was five years old.

12. _____ do you want to go home?

Write the spelling words three times each.

1. wheel _____ _____

_____

2. while _____ _____

_____

3. chin _____ _____

_____

4. chase _____ _____

_____

5. why _____ _____

_____

6. whisper _____

_____

_____

7. branch _____ _____

   _____

8. teach _____ _____

   _____

9. inch _____ _____

   _____

10. watch _____ _____

    _____

11. catch _____ _____

    _____

12. child _____ _____

    _____

Unit 21

1. prize
2. proud
3. princess
4. present
5. pretend
6. pretty
7. drive
8. drove
9. dress
10. drink
11. dream
12. driver

Each of these spelling words begins with a *pr* or *dr* consonant cluster.

prize   proud   princess   present   pretend   pretty

drive   drove   dress   drink   dream   driver

A. Write the spelling words that begin with the consonant cluster **pr.**

1. _____ 2. _____

3. _____ 4. _____

5. _____ 6. _____

B. Write the spelling words that begin with the consonant cluster **dr.**

1. _____ 2. _____

3. _____ 4. _____

5. _____ 6. _____

C. Write the spelling words that have a long **i** sound.

1. _____ 2. _____

3. _____

D. Write the two-syllable spelling word that begins with **dr.**

_____

A. Write the spelling word for each dictionary respelling.

1. (prīz) _____ 2. (drĭngk) _____

3. (drĕs) _____ 4. (drīv) _____

5. (drōv) _____ 6. (drēm) _____

7. (prĭn′ sĕs) _____

8. (prĕz′ ənt) _____

B. Write these words in syllables. Put hyphens between the syllables. Use your spelling dictionary.

1. princess _____

2. driver _____

3. present _____

4. pretty _____

5. pretend _____

C. Write the spelling word that goes with each meaning.

1. feeling great pride _____

2. to make believe _____

3. a thought you have while you are asleep _____

Write a spelling word to complete each sentence.

1. Little girls like to _____ dolls are real babies.

2. Ryan _____ his car to school.

3. Did you win the first place _____?

4. _____ Diana had a beautiful wedding dress.

5. Vickie had a weird _____ while she was taking a nap.

6. The little girl was very _____.

7. I do not like to wrap a _____.

8. Lynn wore a blue _____ to the wedding.

9. I love to _____ milk.

10. Lynn likes to _____ a big van.

11. The _____ should always be careful when it's raining.

12. We should be _____ of our accomplishments.

Write the spelling words three times each.

1. prize _____ _____

_____

2. proud _____ _____

_____

3. princess _____

_____

_____

4. present _____ _____

_____

5. pretend _____ _____

_____

6. pretty _____ _____

_____

7. drive _____ _____

_____

8. drove _____ _____

_____

9. dress _____ _____

_____

10. drink _____ _____

_____

11. dream _____ _____

_____

12. driver _____

_____

_____

Unit 22

1. glad
2. glass
3. glue
4. glove
5. climb
6. clothes
7. clock
8. clever
9. black
10. block
11. blow
12. blanket

Each of these spelling words begins with a *gl*, *cl*, or *bl* consonant cluster.

glad   glass   glue   glove   climb   clothes

clock   clever   black   block   blow   blanket

A. Write the spelling words that begin with the consonant cluster **gl.**

1. _____   2. _____

3. _____   4. _____

B. Write the spelling words that begin with the consonant cluster **cl.**

1. _____   2. _____

3. _____   4. _____

C. Write the spelling words that begin with the consonant cluster **bl.**

1. _____   2. _____

3. _____   4. _____

D. Write the spelling words that have a short **a** sound.

1. _____   2. _____

3. _____   4. _____

A. Write each group of words in alphabetical order. You will need to look at the third and fourth letters.

        block   **black**   **blow**   **blanket**

1. _____ 2. _____

3. _____ 4. _____

        climb   **clock**   **clever**   **clothes**

1. _____ 2. _____

3. _____ 4. _____

        glue   **glad**   **glass**   **glove**

1. _____ 2. _____

3. _____ 4. _____

B. Write two sentences using the words **glad** and **glass**.

1. _____

_____

2. _____

_____

Write a spelling word to complete each sentence.

1. The _____ needed a new battery put in it to continue keeping time properly.

2. Ola dropped the _____, and it broke.

3. Donna liked to _____ the tree when she was young.

4. He needed _____ to fix the model of the ear.

5. We are _____ to only have four days of school this week.

6. Please _____ the candle out before you leave.

7. Clarence was a very _____ boy to make those cabinets for his mother's kitchen.

8. A tiger has _____ and orange stripes.

9. The _____ of wood was heavy.

10. The _____ were in the dryer.

11. I put an extra _____ on me to keep warm.

12. Did that _____ have one finger cut out of it?

Write the spelling words three times each.

1. glad _____   _____

   _____

2. glass _____   _____

   _____

3. glue _____   _____

   _____

4. glove _____   _____

   _____

5. climb _____   _____

   _____

6. clothes _____   _____

   _____

7. clock _____ _____

_____

8. clever _____ _____

_____

9. black _____ _____

_____

10. block _____ _____

_____

11. blow _____ _____

_____

12. blanket _____

_____

_____

Unit 23

1. list 2. lost

3. almost 4. past

5. stand 6. round

7. lock 8. sick

9. pump 10. lump

11. jump 12. stamp

Each of these spelling words end with a consonant cluster.

list   lost   almost   past   stand   round

lock   sick   pump   lump   jump   stamp

A. Write the spelling words that end with the consonant cluster **mp.**

1. _____ 2. _____

3. _____ 4. _____

B. Write the spelling words that end with the consonant cluster **st.**

1. _____ 2. _____

3. _____ 4. _____

C. Write the spelling words that end with the consonant cluster **nd.**

1. _____ 2. _____

D. Write the spelling words that end with the consonant cluster **ck.**

1. _____ 2. _____

E. Write the spelling word that has two syllables.

_____

F. Write two spelling words that begin and end with consonant clusters.

1. _____ 2. _____

A. Write these spelling words in alphabetical order.

    stamp   **pump**   **past**   **list**   **lost**

1. _____ 2. _____

3. _____ 4. _____

5. _____

B. Write the spelling word that goes with each meaning.

1. to be upright on your feet _____

2. ill, not well _____

3. shaped like a ball _____

4. a swelling or bump _____

5. a way of fastening something, usually with a key _____

6. to hop up and down _____

C. Write the word **almost** in syllables. _____

D. Write the word that is an antonym for each of these words.

1. found _____ 2. well _____

Write a spelling word to complete each sentence.

1. You can _____ in the corner for punishment.

2. I made a _____ of things I wanted to do one day.

3. The shape of a circle is _____.

4. It is not fun to be _____ in the woods.

5. When you are _____, you might need to go to a doctor.

6. She slid and got a _____ on her face.

7. Please _____ the door when you leave.

8. She put a _____ on the envelope before mailing it.

9. We drove _____ the store.

10. We are _____ finished with this book.

11. Please do not _____ on the bed when I'm trying to write.

12. You could _____ the handle of the well to get the water to come out.

Write the spelling words three times each.

1. list _____ _____

    _____

2. lost _____ _____

    _____

3. almost _____ _____

    _____

4. past _____ _____

    _____

5. stand _____ _____

    _____

6. round _____ _____

    _____

7. lock _____   _____

_____

8. sick _____   _____

_____

9. pump _____   _____

_____

10. lump _____   _____

_____

11. jump _____   _____

_____

12. stamp _____

_____

_____

Unit 24
Review

Ask teacher for test.

Part 1 Grade _____

Part 2 Grade _____

Part 3 Grade _____

Part 4 Grade _____

Unit 25

1. girl's
2. truck's
3. friend's
4. boy's
5. dog's
6. mom's
7. dad's
8. school's
9. lady's
10. man's
11. rabbit's
12. child's

An 's has been added to each noun to show ownership.

girl's   truck's   friend's   boy's   dog's   mom's

dad's   school's   lady's   man's   rabbit's   child's

A. Write the spelling words that show ownership by a person.

1. _____ 2. _____

3. _____ 4. _____

5. _____ 6. _____

7. _____ 8. _____

B. Write the spelling words that show ownership by an animal.

1. _____ 2. _____

C. Write the spelling word that shows ownership for a vehicle.

_____

D. Write the spelling word that has double consonants.

_____

E. Write the spelling words that have two syllables.

1. _____ 2. _____

A. Write the spelling word for each dictionary respelling.

1. (frĕndz) _____

2. (skülz) _____

3. (trŭks) _____

4. (lā′ dēz) _____

B. Some letters are missing from these words. Fill in the missing letters.

1. d _____ g's 2. _____ _____ m's

3. _____ rie _____ d's 4. b _____ _____'s

5. l _____ d _____'s 6. g _____ rl's

C. Write the form of these words that shows ownership.

1. rabbit _____

2. man _____

3. child _____

4. dad _____

D. Write the word that is an antonym for each word.

1. girl's _____

2. lady's _____

3. dad's _____

A. Write the spelling word that belongs in each sentence.

1. The shoes that belong to the lady are blue.

    The _____ shoes are blue.

2. The car that belonged to my mom was blue.

    My _____ car was blue.

3. The sweater that belongs to the dog is small.

    The _____ sweater is small.

4. The door to the school was locked.

    The _____ door was locked.

5. The van that belonged to my friend was red.

    My _____ van was red.

6. The muffler that belonged to the truck was loud.

    The _____ muffler was loud.

7. The fur on the rabbit was white.

    The _____ fur was white.

B. Unscramble these words.

8. nma's _____ 9. rigl's _____

10. yob's _____ 11. hcldi's _____

12. add's _____

Write the spelling words three times each.

1. girl's _____ _____

   _____

2. truck's _____ _____

   _____

3. friend's _____ _____

   _____

4. boy's _____ _____

   _____

5. dog's _____ _____

   _____

6. mom's _____ _____

   _____

7. dad's _____   _____

   _____

8. school's _____   _____

   _____

9. lady's _____   _____

   _____

10. man's _____   _____

    _____

11. rabbit's _____

    _____

    _____

12. child's _____   _____

    _____

Unit 26

1. kinder
2. harder
3. fresher
4. faster
5. greener
6. sweeter
7. kindest
8. hardest
9. freshest
10. fastest
11. greenest
12. sweetest

The words in this unit that end with the *er* suffix compare two nouns. The words that end with the *est* suffix compare more than two nouns.

kinder   harder   fresher   faster   greener   sweeter

kindest   hardest   freshest   fastest   greenest   sweetest

A. The word **kinder** means "more kind." Write the spelling words that have the suffix **er**.

1. _____ 2. _____

3. _____ 4. _____

5. _____ 6. _____

B. The word **kindest** means "most kind." Write the spelling words that have the suffix **est**.

1. _____ 2. _____

3. _____ 4. _____

5. _____ 6. _____

C. Write the spelling words that begin with the consonant cluster **gr**.

1. _____ 2. _____

D. Write the spelling words that begin with the consonant cluster **sw**.

1. _____ 2. _____

E. Write the spelling words that begin with the consonant cluster **fr**.

1. _____ 2. _____

A. Write the spelling word that goes with each meaning.

1. more difficult _____

2. most kind _____

3. newest _____

4. quicker _____

B. Write the spelling word that means the opposite of each word.

1. easiest _____ 2. meaner _____

3. slowest _____ 4. older _____

C. One spelling word in each group is not spelled correctly. Write the word correctly.

1. grener   harder   fresher   _____

2. kinder   freser   greenest   _____

3. hardest   sweter   fastest   _____

4. kindest   freshest   seetest   _____

5. hader   kinder   greener   _____

Write the spelling word that belongs in each sentence.

1. I can run fast. James can run _____ than I can, but we are not the _____ runners in the world.

2. Our grass is green now, but it was _____ in the summer. It is probably _____ in July.

3. I try to be a kind person. Ms. Salmon is _____ than I am. I believe Minnie is the _____ person I know.

4. Some people think spelling is a hard subject. Others think English is _____. However, many people think math is the _____ subject in school.

5. I like fresh oranges. The bananas were _____ than the apples. In fact, the bananas were the _____ fruit of all.

6. Cake is sweet. Some cookies are _____ than cake. No-bake cookies are probably the _____ of all.

Write the spelling words two times each.

1. kinder _____

   _____

2. harder _____

   _____

3. fresher _____

   _____

4. faster _____

   _____

5. greener _____

   _____

6. sweeter _____

   _____

7. kindest _____

_____

8. hardest _____

_____

9. freshest _____

_____

10. fastest _____

_____

11. greenest _____

_____

12. sweetest _____

_____

Unit 27

1. letting
2. stopped
3. stepped
4. clapped
5. getting
6. sitting
7. grinned
8. rubbed
9. hopped
10. popped
11. begging
12. flopped

Suffixes have been added to these words. The last letter of each base word has been doubled before the suffix *ed* or *ing* was added.

letting   stopped stepped clapped getting   sitting

grinned rubbed hopped popped begging flopped

A. Write a spelling word to solve the puzzle.

   1. grin + n + ed = _____

   2. stop + p + ed = _____

   3. step + p + ed = _____

   4. clap + p + ed = _____

   5. get + t + ing = _____

B. Vowels are missing in these spelling words, Fill in the missing vowels.

   1. gr ____ nn ____ d   2. h ____ pp ____ d

   3. l ____ tt ____ ng   4. s ____ tt ____ ng

   5. r ____ bb ____ d   6. p ____ pp ____ d

   7. b ____ gg ____ ng   8. fl ____ pp ____ d

C. Write the spelling words that begin with a consonant cluster.

   1. _____ 2. _____

   3. _____ 4. _____

   5. _____

A. Dictionaries usually list only the base form of words ending with **ing** and **ed**. Write the entry word (base word) for each of these spelling words.

1. popped _____   2. rubbed _____

3. letting _____   4. stepped _____

5. sitting _____   6. hopped _____

B. One word in each set is misspelled. Write the word correctly.

1. letting   grined   popped   _____

2. stepped claped   flopped   _____

3. rubed   sitting stopped   _____

4. getting hopped   beging   _____

C. Write the spelling word that fits each definition.

1. make a short, sharp sound ___ ___ ___ ___ ___ ___

2. kept from moving ___ ___ ___ ___ ___ ___ ___

3. what you do when going up stairs ___ ___ ___ ___ ___ ___ ___

4. jumped up and down ___ ___ ___ ___ ___ ___

5. smiled broadly ___ ___ ___ ___ ___ ___ ___

A. Use the code to find each spelling word.

a	b	c	d	e	f	g	h	i	l	n
1	2	3	4	5	6	7	8	9	10	11

o	p	r	s	t	u
12	13	14	15	16	17

1. $15 + 9 + 16 + 16 + 9 + 11 + 7$ _____

2. $15 + 16 + 5 + 13 + 13 + 5 + 4$ _____

3. $7 + 14 + 9 + 11 + 11 + 5 + 4$ _____

4. $10 + 5 + 16 + 16 + 9 + 11 + 7$ _____

5. $13 + 12 + 13 + 13 + 5 + 4$ _____

6. $3 + 10 + 1 + 13 + 13 + 5 + 4$ _____

7. $6 + 10 + 12 + 13 + 13 + 5 + 4$ _____

8. $7 + 5 + 16 + 16 + 9 + 11 + 7$ _____

9. $14 + 17 + 2 + 2 + 5 + 4$ _____

10. $8 + 12 + 13 + 13 + 5 + 4$ _____

11. $2 + 5 + 7 + 7 + 9 + 11 + 7$ _____

12. $15 + 16 + 12 + 13 + 13 + 5 + 4$ _____

Write the spelling words two times each.

1. letting _____

   _____

2. stopped _____

   _____

3. stepped _____

   _____

4. clapped _____

   _____

5. getting _____

   _____

6. sitting _____

   _____

7. grinned _____

_____

8. rubbed _____

_____

9. hopped _____

_____

10. popped _____

_____

11. begging _____

_____

12. flopped _____

_____

Unit 28

1. foxes
2. boxes
3. watches
4. matches
5. glasses
6. inches
7. dresses
8. wishes
9. classes
10. brushes
11. branches
12. dishes

These spelling words are plurals. An *es* was added to words ending with *x*, *ch*, *ss*, *sh*, or *tch*.

foxes   boxes   watches   matches   glasses   inches

dresses   wishes   classes   brushes   branches   dishes

A. Write the spelling words that have base words ending with **x.**

1. _____   2. _____

B. Write the spelling words that have base words ending with **ch** or **tch**.

1. _____   2. _____

3. _____   4. _____

C. Write the spelling words that have base words ending with **ss**.

1. _____   2. _____

3. _____

D. Write the spelling words that have base words ending with **sh**.

1. _____   2. _____

3. _____

A. Write the spelling word that goes with each meaning.

1. containers with four sides _____

2. tools used for cleaning or sweeping _____

3. groups of students in a school _____

4. desires _____

5. small sticks used to start a fire _____

6. small animals that look like a dog _____

7. things to drink from _____

8. the part of a tree which holds leaves _____

9. things to eat from _____

10. small units of measurement _____

11. things worn to tell time _____

12. garments worn by women _____

B. Write the spelling word that rhymes with each word.

1. classes _____

2. wishes _____

3. boxes _____

Write the spelling word that belongs in each sentence.

1. Paint _____ are used to paint a picture.

2. There are twelve _____ in a foot.

3. _____ can be very dangerous animals.

4. There are many _____ in the school.

5. You may use _____ to light the candles.

6. We drink water from _____.

7. There were many _____ on the tree.

8. Some children have many _____ for Christmas.

9. Lynn has many _____ in her closet.

10. We looked for many _____ to pack his things.

11. We bought _____ for his children for Christmas.

12. We bought some new _____ for Donna to use in her kitchen.

Write the spelling words two times each.

1. foxes _____

   _____

2. boxes _____

   _____

3. watches_____

   _____

4. matches_____

   _____

5. glasses _____

   _____

6. inches _____

   _____

7. dresses _____

_____

8. wishes _____

_____

9. classes _____

_____

10. brushes _____

_____

11. branches _____

_____

12. dishes _____

_____

Unit 29

1. nearly
2. mostly
3. slowly
4. bravely
5. partly
6. yearly
7. softly
8. clearly
9. loudly
10. badly
11. lonely
12. sadly

These spelling words end with the *ly* suffix.

nearly   mostly   slowly   bravely   partly   yearly

softly   clearly   loudly   badly   lonely   sadly

A. Add the suffix **ly** to each base word to make a spelling word.

1. loud _____   2. soft _____

3. bad _____   4. part _____

5. clear _____   6. year _____

7. sad _____   8. near _____

9. most _____ 10. brave _____

11. lone _____ 12. slow _____

B. Write the spelling words that have the long **e** sound in the base word.

1. _____   2. _____

3. _____

C. Write the spelling word that has a long **a** sound.

_____

D. Write the spelling word that has the **a** controlled by an **r** sound.

_____

A. Write the spelling word for each dictionary respelling.

1. (mōst′ lē) _____

2. (nēr′ lē) _____

3. (brāv′ lē) _____

4. (pärt′ lē) _____

5. (slō′ lē) _____

6. (sôft′ lē) _____

B. One word in each row is misspelled. Write the word correctly.

1. neirly slowly bravely _____

2. cleerly loudly badly _____

3. badely lonely yearly _____

4. softly sadely partly _____

C. Write the word that goes with each meaning.

1. in a soft way _____

2. once a year _____

3. all alone _____

4. in a loud way _____

Write the spelling word that belongs in each sentence.

1. A turtle moves very _____.

2. You should get your eyes tested _____.

3. Rub the rabbit's fur very _____.

4. You could hear the women's voices because they talked so

_____.

5. David was taken to the hospital because he was _____ hurt.

6. The man _____ jumped into the water to save the

person.

7. Jimmy cried so _____ after he heard his pet

rooster had died.

8. I could not see _____ while driving in the rain.

9. When there are just a few clouds in the sky, we say it is

_____ cloudy.

10. When there are many clouds in the sky, we say it is

_____ cloudy.

11. The man seemed very _____ after his wife died.

12. Is it _____ time to get ready to go home?

Write the spelling words two times each.

1. nearly _____

   _____

2. mostly _____

   _____

3. slowly _____

   _____

4. bravely _____

   _____

5. partly _____

   _____

6. yearly _____

   _____

7. softly _____

_____

8. clearly _____

_____

9. loudly _____

_____

10. badly _____

_____

11. lonely_____

_____

12. sadly _____

_____

Unit 30
Review

Ask teacher for test.

Part 1 Grade _____

Part 2 Grade _____

Part 3 Grade _____

Part 4 Grade _____

Unit 31

1. loud
2. out
3. house
4. count
5. sound
6. mouse
7. town
8. tower
9. howl
10. flower
11. owl
12. how

These spelling words have the *ou* diphthong heard in *out* spelled by the letters *ou* or *ow*.

loud   out   house   count   sound   mouse

town   tower   howl   flower   owl   how

A. Write the spelling words in which the vowel sound you hear in **house** is spelled **ou**.

1. _____ 2. _____

3. _____ 4. _____

5. _____ 6. _____

B. Write the spelling words in which the vowel sound you hear in **house** is spelled **ow**.

1. _____ 2. _____

3. _____ 4. _____

5. _____ 6. _____

C. Write the spelling words that have two syllables.

1. _____ 2. _____

D. Write the spelling word that rhymes with each of these words.

1. house _____ 2. flower _____

3. owl _____

A. Write the spelling word for each meaning.

1. to name numbers in order _____

2. very noisy _____

3. a small city _____

4. a noise _____

5. a small rodent _____

6. a kind of bird _____

7. a building in which to live _____

8. the colorful part of a plant _____

B. Letters are missing in these spelling words. Fill in the missing letters.

1. _____ _____ t   2. h _____ _____

3. t _____ _____ er   4. h _____ _____ l

C. Write these words in alphabetical order.

    sound   count   flower   mouse

1. _____   3. _____

2. _____   4. _____

Write the spelling word that belongs in each sentence.

1. The _____ was for rent.

2. A rose is a _____.

3. The _____ of Marty's piano playing was beautiful.

4. Sometimes Byron plays the drums too _____.

5. Do not go _____ of the house when it is night.

6. _____ do you make a lemon pie?

7. I do not like to see a _____ running across my kitchen floor.

8. The _____ of one hundred was small.

9. Can you _____ to three hundred?

10. A wolf can _____ loudly.

11. An _____ sounds like it says "Who."

12. He liked to climb the fire _____.

Write the spelling words three times each.

1. loud _____ _____

   _____

2. out _____ _____

   _____

3. house _____ _____

   _____

4. count _____ _____

   _____

5. sound _____ _____

   _____

6. mouse _____ _____

   _____

7. town _____ _____

_____

8. tower _____ _____

_____

9. howl _____ _____

_____

10. flower _____ _____

_____

11. owl _____ _____

_____

12. how _____ _____

_____

Unit 32

1. tooth
2. who
3. roof
4. fruit
5. balloon
6. juice
7. root
8. blue
9. tool
10. flew
11. broom
12. knew

These spelling words have the vowel sound heard in **boot** spelled by the letters **oo**, **o**, **ui**, **ue** or **ew**.

tooth   who   roof   fruit   balloon   juice

root   blue   tool   flew   broom   knew

A. Write the spelling words that have the vowel sound you hear in **boot** spelled with the letters **oo**.

1. _____ 2. _____

3. _____ 4. _____

5. _____ 6. _____

B. Write the spelling words that have the vowel sound you hear in **boot** spelled with the letters **ui**.

1. _____ 2. _____

C. Write the spelling words that have the vowel sound you hear in **boot** spelled with the letters **ew**.

1. _____ 2. _____

D. Write the spelling word that has the vowel sound you hear in **boot** spelled with the letter **o**.

_____

E. Write the spelling word that has the vowel sound you hear in **boot** spelled with the letters **ue**.

_____

A. Write the spelling word for each dictionary respelling.

1. (früt) _____

2. (tül) _____

3. (jüs) _____

4. (rüt) _____

5. (hü) _____

6. (flü) _____

7. (bə lün′) _____

8. (brüm) _____

9. (nü) _____

B. Write a spelling word that is a homophone for each word.

1. blew _____

2. new _____

C. Write the spelling word that goes with each meaning.

1. the top covering of a house _____

2. one of the white bony parts in the mouth used for chewing _____

3. a toy filled with air _____

Write the spelling word that belongs in each sentence.

1. Did you know that a beautiful _____ can be harmed by decay?

2. Decay can start in the _____ of a tooth.

3. You can use your toothbrush as a _____ to keep your teeth from decaying.

4. Will you be a person _____ stops your teeth from decaying?

5. Drinking _____ or eating _____ might not be good for your teeth.

6. The children could have seen the hot air _____ from the _____ of the house.

7. The balloons _____ high in the sky.

8. We _____ it was the day for the balloon race.

9. The girl was wearing a _____ skirt in the picture.

10. People could fly in a basket under a balloon but not on a _____.

Write the spelling words three times each.

1. tooth _____ _____

   _____

2. who _____ _____

   _____

3. roof _____ _____

   _____

4. fruit _____ _____

   _____

5. balloon _____

   _____

   _____

6. juice _____ _____

   _____

7. root _____ _____

   _____

8. blue _____ _____

   _____

9. tool _____ _____

   _____

10. flew _____ _____

    _____

11. broom_____ _____

    _____

12. knew _____ _____

    _____

Unit 33

1. haircut
2. cowgirl
3. anyone
4. carport
5. icebox
6. sailboat
7. inside
8. bedtime
9. everyone
10. fireside
11. tablecloth
12. waterfall

These spelling words are **compound words**. A compound word is formed by putting two words together.

haircut	cowgirl	anyone	carport
icebox	sailboat	inside	bedtime
everyone	fireside	tablecloth	waterfall

A. Write the spelling words that have the word **one** in them.

1. _____ 2. _____

B. Write the spelling words that have the word **side** in them.

1. _____ 2. _____

C. Write the spelling words that start with the letter **c**.

1. _____ 2. _____

D. Write the spelling words that have three syllables.

1. _____ 2. _____

3. _____ 4. _____

E. Write the spelling words that are made by joining these words.

1. hair + cut _____

2. sail + boat _____

3. ice + box _____

4. bed + time _____

A. Write the spelling word for each dictionary respelling.

1. (kou′ gėrl) _____

2. (bĕd′ tīm) _____

3. (ĕn′ ē wŭn) _____

4. (ĭn sīd′) _____

5. (hãr′ kŭt) _____

6. (fīr′ sīd) _____

B. Write the compound word that goes with each meaning.

1. a place to park a car _____

2. a refrigerator _____

3. a boat moved by the wind _____

4. all of the people _____

5. a cloth to put over a table _____

6. a place beside a fire _____

7. a place where water flows over rocks

_____

Match the words in Box A and Box B to make compound words.

Box A					
ice	any	car	bed	cow	in
sail	fire	table	hair	water	every

Box B					
one	side	fall	box	cut	time
girl	boat	side	one	cloth	port

1. _____
2. _____
3. _____
4. _____
5. _____
6. _____
7. _____
8. _____
9. _____
10. _____
11. _____
12. _____

Write the spelling words two times each.

1. haircut _____

   _____

2. cowgirl_____

   _____

3. anyone _____

   _____

4. carport _____

   _____

5. icebox _____

   _____

6. sailboat _____

   _____

7. inside _____

_____

8. bedtime _____

_____

9. everyone _____

_____

10. fireside _____

_____

11. tablecloth _____

_____

12. waterfall _____

_____

Unit 34

1. our
2. hour

3. I
4. eye

5. its
6. it's

7. buy
8. by

9. one
10. won

11. here
12. hear

Homophones are words that sound alike, but have different meanings, and are spelled differently.

our   hour   I   eye   its   it's

buy   by   one   won   here   hear

A. Write the spelling word that is a homophone for each word.

1. I _____ 2. its _____

3. by _____ 4. one _____

5. our _____ 6. here _____

B. Write the spelling word that is the contraction for **it is**.

_____

C. Write the spelling word that begins and ends with the letter **e**.

_____

D. Write the spelling words that have the long **i** sound.

1. _____ 2. _____

3. _____ 4. _____

E. Write the spelling word that names a number.

_____

A. Write these spelling words in alphabetical order.

our	buy	one	its	here
eye	won	by	hear	hour

1. _____   6. _____

2. _____   7. _____

3. _____   8. _____

4. _____   9. _____

5. _____   10. _____

B. Write the spelling word that goes with each meaning.

1. the contraction for **it is** _____

2. 60 minutes _____

3. belonging to it _____

4. to give money _____

5. near _____

C. Write the two spelling words that would come between these guide words in a dictionary.

on - out _____   _____

Circle the correct spelling word in parenthesis that belongs in each sentence.

1. Vickie (won, one) the spelling bee.

2. Can you come to (hour, our) house?

3. (It's, Its) past seven o'clock at night.

4. Did you (hear, here) the teacher call your name?

5. Put the chair (buy, by) the table.

6. Please put the basket (here, hear).

7. He bought (won, one) candy bar for me.

8. The boy's (I, eye) was hurting.

9. In one (hour, our) it will be time to get ready for bed.

10. You may pet the dog, but don't pull (it's, its) tail.

11. (I, Eye) like to sleep late on Saturday.

12. Please (buy, by) me a laptop computer.

Write the spelling words three times each.

1. our _____ _____

   _____

2. hour _____ _____

   _____

3. I _____ _____

   _____

4. eye _____ _____

   _____

5. its _____ _____

   _____

6. it's _____ _____

   _____

7. buy _____   _____

   _____

8. by _____   _____

   _____

9. one _____   _____

   _____

10. won _____   _____

    _____

11. here _____   _____

    _____

12. hear _____   _____

    _____

Unit 35

1. who'll
2. we've
3. isn't
4. you'll
5. what'll
6. didn't
7. you've
8. won't
9. hasn't
10. hadn't
11. couldn't
12. shouldn't

A **contraction** is a shortened form of two words. An apostrophe (') replaces letters that are missing.

who'll   we've   isn't   you'll   what'll   didn't

you've   won't   hasn't   hadn't   couldn't   shouldn't

A. Write the spelling words that are contractions in which **not** has been shortened.

1. _____   2. _____

3. _____   4. _____

5. _____   6. _____

7. _____

B. Write the spelling words that are contractions in which the verb **will** has been shortened.

1. _____   2. _____

3. _____

C. Write the spelling words that are contractions in which the verb **have** has been shortened.

1. _____   2. _____

D. Write the spelling words that start with a **w**.

1. _____   2. _____

3. _____   4. _____

Write the spelling word that belongs in each sentence.

1. _____ have to get up early in the morning.

2. It _____ time to go to bed yet.

3. _____ fix me some ice cream?

4. _____ you get to school on time every day?

5. _____ we do for room in the refrigerator if we buy too many groceries?

6. _____ been living in this house for a long time.

7. _____ you like to go to the zoo with us?

8. I _____ go across the monkey bars.

9. Lee _____ called me for a long time.

10. _____ been doing better with your reading.

11. _____ we eat lunch before noon?

12. She _____ ever touched a baby lion.

Write the spelling words two times each.

1. who'll _____

   _____

2. we've _____

   _____

3. isn't _____

   _____

4. you'll _____

   _____

5. what'll _____

   _____

6. didn't _____

   _____

7. you've _____

_____

8. won't _____

_____

9. hasn't _____

_____

10. hadn't _____

_____

11. couldn't _____

_____

12. shouldn't _____

_____

Unit 36
Review

Ask teacher for test.

Part 1 Grade _____

Part 2 Grade _____

Part 3 Grade _____

Part 4 Grade _____

Spelling Glossary Pronunciations

ă cat map

ā age, race

ä father, calm

ã care, air

ĕ red, bed

ē eat, he

ė mother, heard

ĭ is, it

ī ice, ride

ŏ hot, cot

ō over, go

ô ball, caught

oi oil, boy

ou house, out

ŭ up, cup
ū use, few
ü rule, move

ə represents.
a in about
e in taken
i in pencil
o in lemon
u in circus

Aa

a-fraid(ə frād′) *adj.* fearful
I am afraid of big dogs.

a-go(ə gō′) *adj.* in the past
I went to that school a long time ago.

a-head(ə hĕd′) *adv.* Straight in front of
Sometimes James walks ahead of me.

air(ãr) *n.* the gases that we breathe
The air is cool today.

al-most(ŏl mōst) *adv.* nearly
Jimmy was almost eleven years old.

al-read-y((ŏl rĕd′ ē) *adv.* before now
I have already gone to the grocery.

an-y-one(ĕn′ ē wŭn) *pron.* any person
Anyone can take the trash out.

ap-ple(ăp′ əl) *n.* the firm fleshy fruit of a tree grown in temperate regions, usually red, yellow, or green
We gathered apples that had fallen to the ground.

a-sleep(ə slēp′) *adj.* not awake
I should have been asleep at midnight.

a-way(ə-wā′) *adv.* not at home
We were away at 6:00 P.M.

Bb

bad-ly(băd′ lē) *adv.* in a bad manner
Doug was hurt badly in the wreck.

bal-loon(bə lün′) *n.* a toy filled with air
I had blue balloons for decorations.

bear(bãr) *n.* a big, clumsy animal with coarse hair and a short tail
I did not want to see a bear in my yard.

bed-time(bĕd′ tīm) *n.* time to go to bed
She called when it was past my bedtime.

be-gan(bē găn′) *v.* did begin
I began to drive the van.

beg(bĕg) *v.* to ask pleadingly
begged, begging
We can get a job so that we do not have to beg.

bird(bėrd) *n.* a flying animal
A robin is a bird.

bit(bĭt) *n.* a small piece of something
I ate a bit of the cake.

birth-day(bėrth – dā) *n.* the day on which a person was born
His birthday is July 4.

black(blăk) *adj.* the opposite of white
Clarence wears black shoes.

blanket

blan-ket(blăng′ kĭt) *n.* a soft, heavy covering used to keep people warm
It was cold this morning, so I got another blanket.

blend (blĕnd) *v.* to mix thoroughly
Make sure you blend the cake mix well.

bless(blĕs) *v.* to praise
We should bless the Lord.

block(blŏk) *n.* a chunk of wood
The blocks had letters on them.

blow(blō) *v.* to move air quickly
You can blow air into a balloon.

blue(blü) *adj.* a color the same as the sky
We have blue carpet in the school.

board(bôrd) *n.* a broad thin piece of wood
James bought boards to make the deck.

boat(bōt) *n.* a small open vessel
We took a ride in the boat.

born(bôrn) *v.* brought forth
The baby should be born soon.

box(bŏks) *n.* a wood or paper container with four sides. *pl. boxes*
I gave Frankie two boxes.

brunch

boy's(boiz) *adj.* belonging to a boy
The boy's pants were brown.

branch(brănch) *n.* the part of a tree that has the leaves. *pl. branches*
Doug stood under the tree branches.

brave-ly(brāv′ lē) *adv.* in a brave way
He bravely petted the black dog.

break-fast(brĕk′ fəst) *n.* the first meal of the day
I ate a boiled egg for breakfast.

breath(brĕth) *n.* air drawn into and forced out of the lungs
Sometimes Frankie needs help to get his breath.

bright(brīt) *adj.* giving much light
The sun is very bright.

broke (brōk) *v.* did break
I broke a glass bowl.

broom(brüm) *n.* a tool used for cleaning a floor
I swept the floor with a broom.

brunch (brŭnch) *n.* a combined breakfast and lunch
We can eat brunch instead of two meals.

brush

brush(brŭsh) *n.* a tool used for cleaning, sweeping, painting, or for getting tangles out of long hair
Always clean the brush when you are finished. *pl. brushes*

burn(bėrn) *v.* to be on fire
I want him to burn the trash.

bush(bush) *n.* a small woody plant smaller than a tree
The car ran over the bush.

but-ter(bŭt′ ər) *n.* a yellowish dairy product
You can put butter on your toast.

buy(bī) *v.* to give money for
Will you buy me some candy?

by(bī) *prep.* near something
We stood by the grave.

C c

cage(kāj) *n.* a box with bars to keep animals in
Fred put pigeons in a cage.

camp(kămp) 1. *n.* a place to play games 2. *v.* to live outdoors such as in a tent
We like to camp at Shady Springs Camp.

check

care(kăr) *v.* to watch over someone
Give your dog water to show you care for it.

car-port(kär′ pôrt) *n.* a place to park a car with no door on it and usually attached to a house
Mr. Kays parked his car in his carport.

catch(kăch) *v.* to take and hold something; capture
Can you catch the ball?

cent(sĭnt) *n.* one penny
James found one cent.

cer-tain(sėrt′ ən) *adj.* sure
I am certain that he has left for work.

chair(chăr) *n.* a single seat with a back on it
I am sitting in a chair.

chance(chăns) *n.* an opportunity; a possibility
There is a chance it will snow in January.

change(chānj) *v.* to make different; to put something in the place of another thing
Kevin needs to make a change in his life.

chase(chās) *v.* to run after to catch
I do not want a dog to chase me.

check (chĕk) *v.* an investigation
Please check to see if the cake is done.

child

child(chīld) *n.* a young boy or girl
She is to have a child soon.

child's(chīld's) *adj.* belonging to a child
The child's seat was safe.

chin(chĭn) *n.* the part of the face below the mouth
Donna had a cut on her chin.

church(chėrch) *n.* a building used as a place to worship of God
We go to church three times per week.

cir-cle(sėr′ kəl) *n.* a round shape
Draw a circle around the correct answer.

cir-cus(sėr′ kəs) *n.* a traveling show of acrobats and wild animals
I only went to the circus once.

cit-y(sĭt′ ē) *n.* a large important town where many people live
He works in the city of Louisville.

clap(klăp) *v.* to make a noise by putting the hands together suddenly
clapped
Clap your hands to the music.

class(klăs) *n.* a group of people in a school
There were eight students in the class.
pl. classes

couldn't

clean(klēn) *adj.* not dirty
The cup was clean.

clear-ly(klēr′ lē) *adj.* in a clear way
I could not see clearly in fog.

clev-er(klĕv′ ər) *adj.* smart; intelligent
Doyle was a clever boy.

climb(klīm) *v.* to go up
Donna loved to climb the tree.

clock(klŏk) *n.* a machine that shows time
To what numbers are the hands on the clock pointing?

close(klōz) *v.* to shut something
Please close the door.

clothes(klōz) *n.* garments to wear
Do not wear your best clothes when going outside to play.

clus-ter (klŭs′ tėr) *n.* a bunch
We could eat a cluster of grapes.

coat(kōt) *n.* a piece of outer clothing worn in the winter

could(kud) *v.* was able to do something
I could play the piano.

could-n't(kud′ ənt) *v.* contraction for could not

count

count(kount) *v.* to name numbers in order
Please count the blocks for me.

cow-girl(kou′ gėrl) *n.* a girl who works on a ranch
Cathy could have been a cowgirl because she liked to ride horses.

crash(krăsh) *v.* to break noisily
I hope an airplane does not crash into my house.

crush (krŭsh) *v.* to smash
I crushed the egg shells.

cry(krī) *v.* to weep
I do not want to hear a baby cry.

D d

dad's(dădz) *adj.* belonging to someone's dad
I liked to drive Dad's car.

dan-ger(dăn′ jər) *n.* a chance of harm
There can be danger when walking in the woods.

did-n't(dĭd′ ənt) *v.* contraction for did not
I didn't mean to hurt the child.

dish(dĭsh) *n.* a container meant for holding food. *pl. dishes*

dog's(dŏgz) *adj.* belonging to a dog
The dog's collar was pink.

drop

dol-lar(dŏl ər) *n.* official money for one hundred pennies
I paid one dollar for the piano.

drag-on(drăg′ ən) *n.* a huge make-believe animal that was said to breathe out fire
I would not want to see a dragon.

draw(drô) *v.* to make a picture with a writing instrument
I can draw a fish.

dream(drēm) *n.* a thought that you feel or see while asleep
Frankie had a bad dream that he didn't want to remember.

dress(drĕs) *n.* a garment meant for girls or women
The teacher really liked my dress.
pl. dresses

drink(dringk) *v.* to swallow a liquid
I like to drink chocolate milk.

drive(drīv) *v.* to control a vehicle
I like to drive a big van.

driv-er(drīv′ ər) *n.* a person who drives a vehicle
He was the driver of the white truck.

drop(drŏp) *n.* a bit of liquid
Put a drop of food coloring in the water.

drove(drōv) *v.* did drive
He drove a school bus.

dry(drī) *adj.* having no water
Please dry the dishes.

E e

ear-ly(ėr′ lē) *adv.* not late, before the usual time
Ola was early for her appointment.

earn(ėrn) *v.* to get paid for work
I would like to earn some money.

earth(ėrth) *n.* the planet we live on
The earth is round.

eve-ry-one(ev′ rē wun) *pro.* all of the people
Was everyone in class today?

eye(ī) *n.* the part of the body we see with
She went to the doctor to get her eye checked.

F f

fair(fãr) 1) *n.* a show of things that have been made 2) *adj.* clear or sunny
The weather is not fair today.

fast(făst) *adj.* quick
faster, fastest
The squirrel was running fast.

fawn(fôn) *n.* a young deer
The story said the little boy gave the fawn a drink from his hand.

feel(fēl) *v.* to touch
I like the feel of someone combing my hair.

fence(fĕns) *n.* an outdoor wall around a yard or garden
He has a fence to keep his dogs in the yard.

fire-side(f īr′ sīd) *n.* space around a fireplace
We could sit at the fireside and read books.

first(fėrst) *adj.* before all the others
Watch the traffic light if you are first in line.

flame(flā) *n.* the glowing part of a fire
The flame was bright.

flash(flăsh) *n.* a sudden burst of light
Did you see the flash of lightning?

flew(flü) *v.* past tense of fly
A plane flew over our house.

flop(flŏp) *v.* to flap around clumsily
flopped
A fish might flop if you put it on land.

flower

flow-er(flou′ ər) *n.* a blossom; the part of a plant which produces seeds
I bought bright pink flowers.

flush (flŭsh) *v.* filled to overflowing
Please flush the toilet after you use it.

fly(flī) *v.* to move through the air without touching the ground
I do not have wings, so I can not fly.

fold(fōld) *v.* to bend or double over on itself
Fold your paper in half.

fork(fôrk) *n.* an eating utensil with prongs
You can eat beans with a fork.

fox(fŏks) *n.* a small, wild animal similar to a dog. *pl. foxes*
A fox is a sly creature.

fresh(frĕsh) *adj.* newly made
fresher, freshest
The cookies were fresh.

friend's(frĕndz) *adj.* belonging to a friend
My friend's vehicle is a jeep.

fruit(früt) *n.* the sweet juicy part of a plant that is edible
An apple is a fruit.

good

get(gĕt) *v.* receive
getting
Will you get a cookie for me?

gi-ant(jī′ ənt) *adj.* extremely large
Goliath was a giant.

girl's(gėrlz) *adj.* belonging to a girl
That small desk was the girl's desk.

glad(glăd) *adj.* happy or pleased
I was glad that Patti helped me.

glass(glăs) *n.* a thing to drink from
I put milk in a glass. *pl. glasses*

glide (glīd) *v.* to move smoothly over an area

glim-mer (glĭm′ ėr) *v.* an unsteady light

glob (glŏb) *n.* a large rounded mass
Do not sit in a glob of mud.

glove(glŭv) *n.* a covering for the hand
It is good to put gloves on in winter.

glue(glü) *n.* a substance used to stick things together
We can glue boards together.

good(gud) *adj.* excellent
He did a good job making the deck.

green

green(grēn) *adj.* the color of many growing plants and grass
greener, greenest
She wore a green blouse.

grill(grĭl) *v.* to cook over an open fire
We can grill hotdogs outside.

grin(grĭn) *n.* a broad smile
grinned
Please grin when getting your picture made.

H h

had-n't(hăd′ ənt) *v.* contraction for had not
I hadn't gone to sleep by 10:00 P.M.

hair-cut(hãr′ kŭt) *n.* a trim of the hair on the head
James got a haircut last night.

hard(härd) *adj.* difficult
harder, hardest
The geometry test was not hard.

has-n't(hăz′ ənt) *v.* contraction for has not
She has not talked to me today.

hawk(hôk) *n.* a large bird with a strong, hooked beak, and large curved claws
Hawks were trained to kill other birds.

hop

hay(hā) *n.* grass cut and dried as food for cattle
There were several bails of hay on the trailer.

head(hĕd) *n.* the part of the body above the neck
Frankie had a pain in his head.

hear(hēr) *v.* to get sounds through the ear

heard(hėrd) *v.* past tense of hear
I heard the phone ring.

heav-y(hĕv′ ē) *adj.* weighing a large amount
The piano was very heavy.

hel-lo(hĕ lō′) *n.* a greeting.
I usually say, "Hello," when I answer the phone.

here(hēr) *adv. i*n this place
Abigail is not here.

high(hī) *adj.* not low
The can was on a high shelf.

hold(hōld) *v.* to grasp and keep
I will hold the bowl.

hop(hŏp) *v.* to jump on one foot
hopped
You can hop on the concrete.

horse

horse(hôrs) *n.* a four legged animal with hoofs, a mane, and tail
Fred liked having a horse.

hour(our) *n.* sixty minutes
I was in the class for two hours.

house(hous) *n.* a building for people to live in
Do you want to come to our house?

how(hou) *adv.* the way something is done
How do you bake cookies?

howl(houl) *n.* a loud cry
Some puppies howl at night.

hum(hŭm) *v.* to sing with closed lips
Sometimes I hum if I don't know the words to a song.

hur-ry(hėr′ ē) *v.* to rush
Please hurry to get home.

hurt((hėrt) *v.* to cause pain
I hurt my hand.

hus-band(hŭz′ bănd) *n.* a married man
Edward is Brenda's husband.

I i

I(ī) *pron.* myself
I like ice cream.

jump

ice-box(īs′ bŏks) *n.* another name for a refrigerator
We keep milk in the icebox.

inch(ĭnch) *n.* a measurement that is one-twelfth of a foot. *pl. inches*

in-side(ĭn sīd′) *adj.* indoors
I am inside the house now.

in-stead((ĭn stĕd′) *adv.* in place of
I want to go to Tennessee instead of Illinois.

is-n't(ĭs′ ənt) *v.* contraction for is not.
She isn't too happy with me now.

its(ĭts) *adj.* belonging to it
Do you have its name?

it's(ĭts) contraction for it is
It's a nice day.

J j

jaw(jô) *n.* the lower part of the face
I'm glad my jaw was not broken.

juice(jüs) *n.* the watery part of a fruit
I like to drink orange juice.

jump(jŭmp) *v.* to spring up from something
The boys like to jump on the trampoline.

K k

keep(kēp) *v.* to hold on to
We did not want to keep the trash.

kind(kīnd) *adj.* nice; thoughtful
kinder, kindest
To send those flowers was very kind of him.

knew(nū) *v.* past tense of know
I knew who the visitor was.

L l

la-dy's(lā′ dēz) *adj.* belonging to a lady
The lady's dress was pretty.

land(lănd) *n.* the ground
It rained on the land this morning.

large(lärj) *adj.* big
Louisville is a large city.

law(lô) *n.* a rule to live by
Obey the law, and stay out of trouble.

lawn(lôn) *n.* the green grass around a house
James mowed the lawn.

lead(lĕd) *n.* a gray metal used for pipes
We can use plastic now instead of lead.

leap(lēp) *v.* to jump or spring
Do not leap over the fence.

learn(lėrn) *v.* to gain knowledge
I want to learn to play the guitar.

let(lĕt) *v.* allow; permit
letting
Will you let me go to the store?

lie(lī) *v.* to rest flat on something
Please lie down and get some rest.

light(līt) *adj.* not heavy
The keyboard was light.

list(lĭst) *n.* a serious of words
Please make a list of the spelling words.

load(lōd) 1. *n.* the things that are to be carried 2. *v.* to put in the things that are to be carried
Did you load the wood in the truck?

lock(lŏk) *n.* a thing to fasten or close something
He put a lock on the fence.

lone-ly(lōn′ lē) *adj.* feeling along and wanting company
There are times Linda has felt lonely.

lost(lôst) *v.* did lose
I thought I had lost the money.

loud

loud(loud) *adj.* extremely noisy
The music was loud.

loud-ly(loud′ lē) *adv.* in a loud way
She sang loudly for all to be able to hear.

lump(lŭmp) *n.* 1)a swelling or a bump
 2) a small solid mass with no specific shape
Take a lump of clay and make a bowl.

M m

man's(mănz) *adj.* belonging to a man
That beige coat was a man's coat.

match(măch) *n.* a small stick of wood with a mixture on the end that makes fire when rubbed. *pl. matches*
You can use a match to start a fire.

may-be(mā′ bē) *adv.* possibly or perhaps
If it doesn't rain, maybe we can go outside.

mean(mēn) *adj.* not nice; bad.
Noah was mean to his sister.

mom's(mŏmz) *adj.* belonging to a mother
My mom's car was silver.

more(môr) *adj.* a greater amount
Greg has more money than I do.

most-ly(mōst′ lē) *adv.* almost all
The street is mostly wet this morning.

one

mouse(mous) *n.* a small, usually gray, gnawing animal
There was a mouse in the kitchen.

my(mī) *pron.* belonging to me
My cup is red.

N n

near-ly(nēr′ lē) *adv.* almost
It is nearly 11:00 A.M.

nee-dle(nē′ dəl) *n.* a very slender tool that is sharp at one end and has a hole in the other end for thread to pass through for sewing
I used a needle to sew buttons on a shirt.

night(nīt) *n.* the opposite of day; time when it is dark
We walked up the street one night.

north(nôrth) *n.* the direction a needle points on a compass
Kentucky is north of Tennessee.

nose(nōz) *n.* the part of the face just above the mouth through which we breathe
I can breathe through my nose.

O o

one(wŭn) *n.* a number; a single
I have more one computer.

on-ly(ōn′ lē) *adj.* by itself
Moriah is their only child.

o-pen(ō′ pən) *adj.* not shut
Please open the door for me.

o-range(ôr′ inj) 1) *n.* a round juicy fruit.
2) *adj.* a color that is a mixture of red and yellow.
Oranges are a good source of vitamin C.

our(our) *pron.* belonging to us
Our van is white.

out(out) *adv.* the opposite of in
The man was out of the house.

o-ver(ō′ vər) *prep.* above something
A plane flew over the house.

owl(oul) *n.* a bird with big eyes, a short hooked beak, and hunts for food at night
I heard an owl close to our house.

P p

paid(pād) *v.* did pay

paint(pānt) 1)*v.* to coat with a color
2) *n.* the coloring liquid used to change the color of an object
I used red paint on the piano.

pair(pãr) *n.* two of the same kind
I have a pair of white tennis shoes.

part-ly(pärt′ lē) *adv.* not all the way
The front door is partly open.

past(păst) *adv.* gone by; ended
I have eaten broccoli in the past.

peek(pēk) *v.* to look slyly and quietly
Some children like to peek to see presents early.

peep(pēp) *v.* to look through a small hole

pen-ny(pĕn′ ē) *n.* a piece of money worth one cent
James found a penny.

per-son(pėr′ sən) *n.* a human being
The person knocked on the door.

plain(plān) *adv.* easy to understand; not fancy
The blue dress was plain.

plate (plāt) *n.* a flat thin dish

pond(pŏnd) *n.* a body of water smaller than a lake.
Fred had a pond dug.

pop(pŏp) *v.* to make a short, quick, explosive sound   **popped**
Firecrackers can make a loud pop.

pour(pôr) *v.* cause to flow in a steady stream
Do not pour too much in each glass.

pres-ent(prĕz′ ənt) *n.* a gift
There were many presents for Christmas.

pre-tend(prē tĕnd′) *v.* make believe
Sarah likes to pretend she's a mom.

pret-ty(prĭt′ ē) *adj.* pleasing to see
The banquet dress was very pretty.

prin-cess(prĭn′ sĕs) *n.* the daughter of a king or queen
Princess Diana had blond hair.

prize(prīz) *n.* a reward after competing with others
James hopes to win the prize.

proud(proud) *adj.* thinking well of oneself
Kevin was very proud of himself for getting his degree.

pull(pul) *v.* to draw something toward you
Pull the door toward you.

pump(pŭmp) *n.* a machine that forces a liquid or gas in or out of something
Please pump the gas for me.

R r

rab-bit's(răb′ĭtz) *adj.* belonging to a rabbit
The rabbit's fur was white.

rain(rān) *n.* drops of falling water
Yesterday plenty of rain fell.

ranch(rănch) *n.* a large farm
Lyndon Johnson lived on a ranch.

raw(rô) *adj.* not cooked
I love to eat raw potatoes.

read(rēd) *v.* to get the meaning of words
I like to read small stories.

read(rĕd) *v.* past tense of read
I read most of the book about John Bunyan.

read-y(rĕd′ē) *adj.* prepared for action
I was finally ready to leave.

road(rōd) *n.* a way between places
I walked down the road for exercise.

roar(rôr) *v.* to make a loud noise like a growl
A lion roars.

rock (rŏk) *n.* a mass of stony material
The man dumped rocks into our driveway.

roof

roof(rüf) *n.* the top covering of a building
James put a roof on the house.

root(rüt) *n.* the part of a plant that grows underground; the part of a tooth below the gum.
Baby teeth come out without the root.

round(round) *adj.* shaped like a ball
The planets are round.

rub(rŭb) *v.* to move something back and forth against another object **rubbed**
Do not rub your hand on wet paint.

S s

sad-ly(săd′ lē) *adj.* in a sad way
He sadly walked into the room.

sail-boat(sāl′ bōt) *n.* a boat that is moved by the wind
The Mayflower was a sailboat.

sang(săng) past tense of sing
Janelle sang beautifully.

school's(skülz) *adj.* belonging to a school
The school's piano is red, white, and blue.

shave (shāv) *v.* to make smooth by cutting the hair from

shirt(shėrt) *n.* a garment worn by males over the back and chest
He wore a patriotic shirt.

spend

shock (shŏk) *n.* an electrical charge
Do not put your fingers into the socket if you do not want to feel a shock.

should-n't(shud′ ənt) *v.* contraction for should not
We shouldn't disrespect our parents.

sick(sĭk) *adj.* ill, in poor health

sil-ver(sĭl′ vər) *n.* a shiny grayish metal
Some rings are made of silver.

sir(sėr) *n.* a title of respect for males
You should say, "Yes, sir," when the preacher asked you to do something.

sit(sĭt) *v.* to take a seat **sitting**
Will you sit in the front row?

slaw(slô) *n.* a salad made from chopped cabbage, carrots, and dressing
I love to eat slaw.

slow-ly(slō′ lē) *adv.* in a slow way
The bride walked slowly up the aisle.

soft-ly(sôft′ lē) *adv.* in a soft way
You may touch the baby softly.

sound(sound) *n.* a noise that can be heard

spend(spĕnd) *v.* to pay out
Please do not spend too much money.

splint(splĭnt) *n.* a device to keep an injured part in place temporarily
You can use a splint if you break your leg while walking in the woods.

stair(stãr) *n.* a step *pl. stairs*
Be careful when walking up the stairs.

stamp(stămp) 1) *n.* a piece of paper that you buy to put on mail in order to mail it
2) *v.* to make a loud noise when you put your feet down
Do not forget to put a stamp on your letter.

stand(stănd) *v.* to be upright on one's feet
Please stand until you are ask to be seated.

stare(stãr) *v.* to look at something for a long time
Please do not stare at handicapped people.

state (stāt) *n.* a place where people live and are organized in one government
There are fifty states in the United States.

step(stĕp) *v.* to pick one foot up and put it down again, then do the same to the other
stepped
Please do not step on flowers.

stole (stōl) *v.* did steal
He stole some things from the store.

stood(stüd) *v.* past tense of stand
Karen stood for a long time.

stop(stŏp) *v.* to quit doing something
stopped

stor-y (stôr′ ē) *n.* something that is told to entertain

stove (stōv) *n.* a thing to cook on, which has an oven to be able to bake in.
I baked a cake in my stove.

straw(strô) *n.* a tube used to drink through

sup-per(sŭp′ ər) *n.* the evening meal.
Supper should be ready by 5:00 P.M.

sweet(swēt) *adj.* having a taste like sugar.
sweeter, sweetest
The cookies were very sweet.

T t

ta-ble-cloth(tā′ bəl klŏth) *n.* cloth used for covering a table
I bought Christmas tablecloths for the tables.

teach(tēch) *v.* to help someone learn.
I love to teach math.

thaw(thô) *v.* to melt something that was frozen
The water will thaw if you leave it in the sun.

their

their(thãr) *pron.* belonging to them
That white truck is their truck.

there(thãr) *adv.* in that place
Set the book there.

third(thėrd) *adj.* next after the second
Jordan was her third boy.

thread(thrĕd) *n.* a fine cord used for sewing
Get the brown thread to sew the dress.

tool(tül) *n.* a thing used for working
A rake is a tool for raking leaves.

tooth(tüth) *n.* a hard bonelike part in the mouth used for biting or chewing.
I chipped my tooth.

tow-er(tou′ ər) *n.* a high structure
Some men watch from the tower.

town(toun) *n.* a large group of houses or buildings, smaller than a city
The town had one hundred people.

truck(trŭk) *n.* a strongly built automobile used for hauling things.
James owned a white truck.

turn(tėrn) 1) *n.* a time to do your thing.
  2) *v.* to move around in a circle
Please do not turn around in your seat during a test.

wear

tur-tle(tėr′ təl) *n.* an animal with a soft body which is enclosed in a hard shell.
Did you see a turtle crossing the road?

twin(twĭn) *n.* one of two children born at the same time from the same parents.
Stephanie and Richard were twins.

U u

un-cle(ŭng′ kəl) *n.* the brother of your father or mother.
I had an uncle whose name was Charles.

un-der(ŭn′ dər) *prep.* below
Keep your feet under the table.

un-til(ŭn tĭl′) *prep.* up to that time.
Billy didn't want to wait until night.

W w

watch(wŏch) 1) *n.* a small clock usually worn on the wrist.
2) *v.* to look closely.
pl. watches

wa-ter-fall(wŏ′ tər fôl) *n.* fall of water from a higher place.

wear(wãr) *v.* to have clothes on the body.
A woman should wear dresses.

weather

weath-er(wĕth′ ər) *n.* condition of the air in a place
The weather is cool tonight.

we've(wēv) contraction for we have
We've been at church tonight.

what'll (hwŏt′ əl) contraction for what will
What'll we do if someone buys the house?

wheel (hwēl) *n.* the round part of a bicycle or car that touches the ground
A car has four wheels.

when(hwĕn) *adv.* at what time
When will we be leaving?

where(hwãr) *adv.* in what place
Where will we meet?

while(hwīl) *conj.* during that time
What will we do while we wait?

whis-per(hwĭs′ pər) *v.* to speak very softly
Please whisper to not wake the baby.

who(hü) *pron.* the person that
Who will go with me?

who'll(hül) contraction for who will
Who'll go with us?

worth

why(hwī) *adv.* for what reason
Why did he get into trouble?

wish(wĭsh) *n.* something a person desires
pl. wishes
Clarence wishes to win the contest.

won(wŭn) *v.* past tense of win
Who won the race?

won't(wōnt) contraction for will not
I won't marry him.

wood-en(wud′ ən) *adj.* something made of logs or boards
The bookcase was wooden.

word(wėrd) *n.* a sound or a group of sounds that has meaning
We can spell many words by learning the letter sounds.

work(wėrk) *n.* labor; a job
James has gone to work.

worm(wėrm) *n.* a small animal with no legs used for fishing
I do not like to touch worms.

wor-ry(wėr′ ē) *v.* to be uneasy about something
I worry about James having a wreck.

worth(wėrth) *adj.* having value
The dimes were worth more than ten cents.

Y y

yawn(yŏn) *v.* to open the mouth wide and take a deep breath
I began to yawn when I was tired.

year-ly(yēr′ lē) *adj.* once each year
The Fairdale Fair was held yearly.

you'll(ūl) contraction for you will
You'll be happy if you'll go to church.

you've(ūv) contraction for you have
You've been to the park one time.

Unit 6
Review of lessons 1-5
Part 1
Circle the letter of the correct spelling for the word that belongs in the blank.

1. James could _____ a can with his foot.

    A. cresh   B. cruch   C. crush

2. She ate the red _____.

    A. aple   B. apple   C. appel

3. We like to go to church _____.

    A. cammp   B. camp   C. kamp

4. The Komodo _____ looks like a lizard.

    A. dragoon   B. dragun   C. dragon

5. The _____ had big buffalos.

    A. ranch   B. runch   C. rench

6. I felt a _____ from the lamp.

    A. shock   B. shok   C. shoch

7. We should _____ the Lord with all our soul.

    A. bles   B. bless   C. blass

8. I have a shiny _____.

    A. penny   B. pinny   C. penne

9. Place a _____ of glue on your paper.

    A. globb   B. glob   C. gloob

10. Please _____ to see if we have any milk.

    A. cheak   B. chek   C. check

11. I don't want to hear two cars _____.

    A. cresh   B. crash   C. crach

12. Please _____ the cake mix well.

    A. blend   B. blind   C. blende

13. I saw a _____ of lightning.

    A. flach   B. fash   C. flash

14. Doyle was _____ enough to read the time on the machine.

    A. clevar   B. clevver   C. clever

15. A combined breakfast and lunch is called _____.

    A. brunch   B. bruench   C. brunsh

Unit 6
Review of lessons 1-5
Part 2

Circle the letter of the correct spelling for the word that belongs in the blank.

1. Be _____ and let me help you.

   A. still   B. stil   C. stell

2. The flood water pushed the _____ over.

   A. fense   B. fence   C. fince

3. The _____ had muddy water in it.

   A. pond   B. pand   C. pund

4. The _____ of grapes was big.

   A. clusster   B. kluster   C. cluster

5. It _____ to rain.

   A. begen   B. began   C. beegan

6. Patti cooked food on the _____.

   A. grell   B. grile   C. grill

7. Kevin wore a _____ on his finger.

   A. splent   B. splint   C. spleint

8. Use the water have to _____ the drain.

 A. fluch   B. fluish   C. flush

9. David sold a _____ at the flea market.

 A. rock   B. rok   C. roeck

10. You should _____ plenty of water.

 A. drink   B. drenk   C. dreink

11. She _____ a beautiful song.

 A. song   B. seng   C. sang

12. Missie had a _____ of hope that Matt would graduate.

 A. glimer   B. glimmer   C. glimmar

13. _____ are you coming home?

 A. whin   B. when   C. whene

14. The _____ was hilly in Eastern Kentucky.

 A. lend   B. lande   C. land

15. I did not want to _____ a lot of money on vacation.

 A. spand   B. spind   C. spend

Unit 6
Review of lessons 1-5
Part 3

Circle the letter of the correct spelling for the word that belongs in the blank.

1. Mike drove his _____ up the road.

    A. truk   B. truck   C. truke

2. _____ is not as costly as gold.

    A. sliver   B. silvre   C. silver

3. We like to go to the store named _____ Tree.

    A. Dollar   B. Doller   C. Dollur

4. Stephanie had a _____ brother.

    A. tiwn   B. twin   C. twine

5. Wayne did not come over _____ James called him today.

    A. unntil   B. untill   C. until

6. Please do not _____ the vase.

    A. drop   B. dropp   C. dorp

7. I fixed eggs for _____.

    A. brakfast   B. breakfest   C. breakfast

23

8. I _____ the story "Pilgrim's Progress."

    A. red   B. raed   C. read

9. He had _____ started reading the Bible before we got married.

    A. allready   B. already   C. alredy

10. I quickly got _____ to go.

    A. ready   B. redy   C. raedy

11. I put the _____ through the needle.

    A. thred   B. thread   C. thraed

12. Kevin had a big _____ when he was born.

    A. hed   B. head   C. haed

13. The guide _____ us through the cave.

    A. lad   B. lede   C. lead

14. Lily is a short _____ girl.

    A. heavy   B. hevy   C. haevy

15. He could easily run _____ of me.

    A. ahead   B. ahed   C. aheed

Unit 6
Review of lessons 1-5
Part 4

Circle the letter of the correct spelling for the word that belongs in the blank.

1. The _____ was hot and humid.

   A. weether   B. wether   C. weather

2. Billy called _____ of writing a letter.

   A. instead   B. insted   C. insteed

3. A doctor might ask you to take a deep _____.

   A. breathe   B. breath   C. brethe

4. How _____ Lisa be so mean?

   A. culd   B. coold   C. could

5. Jimmy wanted the _____ picnic table to be painted red, white, and blue.

   A. wooden   B. wudden   C. woulden

6. Vickie went to McDonalds and bought food for _____.

   A. super   B. supper   C. sopper

7. Crystal and James got married, so James is her _____.

   A. husbend   B. husband   C. husbind

8. You could hide an egg behind a _____.

    A. boosh   B. buch   C. bush

9. James is named after his _____ Clarence.

    A. uncle   B. unkle   C. unkel

10. The shoes were _____ the bed.

    A. undre   B. undor   C. under

11. The children _____ for the Pledge of Allegiance.

    A. stud   B. stood   C. studd

12. If you put _____ on bread, you can make toast.

    A. buter   B. buttre   C. butter

13. If you study, you can get a _____ grade.

    A. gud   B. good   C. gudd

14. _____ is the opposite of push.

    A. Pull   B. Pul   C. Pool

15. You can _____ a tune.

    A. hum   B. hume   C. humm

Unit 12
Review of lessons 7-11
Part 1

Circle the letter of the correct spelling for the word that belongs in the blank.

1. Will you _____ for me?

    A. wat   B. wate   C. wait

2. Someone _____ the trailer.

    A. stol   B. stole   C. stolle

3. Did Frankie _____ his beard?

    A. shafe   B. shaeve   C. shave

4. The _____ of the fire was hot.

    A. flame   B. flaim   C. flam

5. We bought a white _____ .

    A. stove   B. stofe   C. stoove

6. I think they like the _____ of Kentucky.

    A. staet   B. state   C. stait

7. Ben likes to _____ down the slide.

    A. glied   B. glid   C. glide

8. If you _____ at someone, they will usually _____ back at you.

    A. smiel   B. smile   C. smil

9. Put the food on the _____.

    A. plate   B. plat   C. plait

10. Who _____ the mirror?

    A. brok   B. broak   C. broke

11. Study the Bible so you can be _____.

    A. wise   B. wiss   C. wis

12. It was hard to see while driving in the _____.

    A. ran   B. rain   C. rane

13. I _____ the bill.

    A. paid   B. paed   C. pade

14. The opposite of black is _____.

    A. whitt   B. whit   C. white

15. Please _____ the door.

    A. cloas   B. close   C. clos

Unit 12
Review of lessons 7-11
Part 2

Circle the letter of the correct spelling for the word that belongs in the blank.

1. Horse eat _____.

    A. hay   B. hae   C. hya

2. I do not like to ride in a _____.

    A. baot   B. bote   C. boat

3. I am _____ of bears.

    A. afrade   B. afrad   C. afraid

4. _____ is the first day of the rest of your life.

    A. todae   B. today   C. to-day

5. Help me _____ the clothes.

    A. fold   B. foed   C. folde

6. _____ the wall white.

    A. pant   B. paint   C. pante

7. The _____ went up the hill.

    A. rode   B. roed   C. road

219

8. _____ inside until the rain stops.

    A. stay   B. stae   C. sty

9. Wear a _____ in winter time.

    A. coat   B. cote   C. cota

10. _____ it will snow on Christmas.

    A. mabe   B. maybe   C. maybee

11. _____ your pencil right.

    A. holed   B. hold   C. holld

12. Put the food on a _____.

    A. trey   B. trae   C. tray

13. The opposite of fancy is _____.

    A. plane   B. plain   C. plan

14. _____ the truck with oranges.

    A. load   B. lode   C. lod

15. Be quiet when the teacher is _____.

    A. awae   B. awey   C. away

Unit 12
Review of lessons 7-11
Part 3

Circle the letter of the correct spelling for the word that belongs in the blank.

1. You should say _____ when you answer the phone.

    A. hellow   B. hello   C. hillo

2. The baby did not want to fall _____.

    A. asleep   B. asleap   C. awsleep

3. A long time _____ we went to Banquet Table.

    A. ago   B. agoe   C. ego

4. A baby chicken makes a sound that sounds like "_____."

    A. pepe   B. peap   C. peep

5. There was _____ one teacher in the room.

    A. only   B. onle   C. onely

6. A bull can be _____.

    A. meen   B. mene   C. mean

7. _____ is the opposite of closed.

    A. opin   B. open   C. opan

8. The dress was _____.

    A. clean   B. clene   C. claen

9. The name of the _____ is Preston.

    A. streat   B. stret   C. street

10. _____ the book.

    A. rede   B. raed   C. read

11. Wiggle your _____ in the water.

    A. to   B. toe   C. toa

12. We went _____ the hill.

    A. over   B. ove   C. ovar

13. Did you _____ the soft towel?

    A. feal   B. feel   C. fell

14. Get the padded _____.

    A. seat   B. seet   C. set

15. Can you _____ across the puddle?

    A. leep   B. lap   C. leap

Unit 12
Review of lessons 7-11
Part 4

Circle the letter of the correct spelling for the word that belongs in the blank.

1. Turn the _____ on.

   A. lite　　　　　　B. light　　　　　　C. lit

2. The _____ is blue with white clouds.

   A. sky　　　　　　B. ski　　　　　　C. scy

3. Do not poke yourself with a _____.

   A. needel　　　　　　B. neadle　　　　　　C. needle

4. Do not _____ into the room when your mom is wrapping gifts.

   A. peek　　　　　　B. peak　　　　　　C. peck

5. The sun is _____.

   A. brite　　　　　　B. brihgt　　　　　　C. bright

6. When a person is sad, they might _____.

   A. cri　　　　　　B. cry　　　　　　C. crie

7. Never tell a _____.

   A. lye　　　　　　B. lie　　　　　　C. lei

8. Always do the _____ thing.

   A. right   B. riet   C. rite

9. You can _____ a kite during the day.

   A. flie   B. fli   C. fly

10. Do not fly a kite at _____.

   A. night   B. nite   C. nitte

11. _____ a tail onto it.

   A. tei   B. tye   C. tie

12. Make sure it is a _____ day.

   A. dri   B. dry   C. drie

13. Fly it _____ in the sky.

   A. hie   B. high   C. hieh

14. _____ school is small.

   A. mie   B. me   C. my

15. We want to _____ it that way.

   A. keep   B. keap   C. kepe

Unit 18
Review of lessons 13-17
Part 1

Circle the letter of the correct spelling for the word that belongs in the blank.

1. The _____ of David and Goliath is fun to read.

    A. store	B. stury	C. story

2. _____ the water into a glass.

    A. pour	B. pure	C. pore

3. Put letters together to make a _____.

    A. werd	B. word	C. wurd

4. Go _____ to get to Canada.

    A. nerth	B. north	C. nroth

5. James put the _____ down on the floor.

    A. board	B. borde	C. bored

6. The baby wanted _____ food.

    A. mour	B. moar	C. more

7. Use a _____ to eat your food.

    A. fourk	B. fork	C. forke

8. Abraham Lincoln was _____ in February.

    A. born   B. borne   C. burn

9. I do not like to touch a _____.

    A. werm   B. werme   C. worm

10. Goliath was tall, and David was _____.

    A. sort   B. shourt   C. short

11. A lion can _____.

    A. rore   B. roar   C. raor

12. A _____ can gallop.

    A. hourse   B. hors   C. horse

13. You should finish your school _____ at school.

    A. work   B. werk   C. wurk

14. I want to make a high _____ on every test.

    A. score   B. scor   C. scour

15. Do you like to go to the _____?

    A. stor   B. store   C. sture

Unit 18
Review of lessons 13-17
Part 2

Circle the letter of the correct spelling for the word that belongs in the blank.

1. You go to school to _____.

    A. learn   B. lern   C. lurne

2. The _____ is the planet on which we live.

    A. eurth   B. erth   C. earth

3. Jesus loves me, so I should not _____.

    A. worry   B. wurry   C. worre

4. Go to church on the _____ day of the week.

    A. ferst   B. first   C. furst

5. Tuesday is the _____ day of the week.

    A. therd   B. third   C. thurd

6. A _____ gave food to Elijah.

    A. burd   B. berd   C. bird

7. The dinner meal was served _____.

    A. early   B. erly   C. urly

8. We _____ going to eat.

    A. where   B. wure   C. were

9. You can _____ some money.

    A. urn   B. earn   C. erne

10. December 5 is my _____.

    A. burthday   B. birthday   C. berthday

11. Only one _____ should be talking.

    A. persun   B. purson   C. person

12. Earl word a red _____.

    A. shert   B. shirt   C. shurt

13. I _____ the preacher talking.

    A. heard   B. herd   C. hard

14. It is proper to say, "_____," when talking to a man.

    A. sir   B. ser   C. shir

15. A dollar is _____ one hundred pennies.

    A. werth   B. wirth   C. worth

Unit 18
Review of lessons 13-17
Part 3

Circle the letter of the correct spelling for the word that belongs in the blank.

1. A _____ was on the road.

    A. tertle   B. turtle   C. turtel

2. You can learn about God in _____.

    A. cherch   B. church   C. chirch

3. Sit down in the _____.

    A. chare   B. chere   C. chair

4. How many _____ are there to climb?

    A. stairs   B. steres   C. stares

5. You should _____ clean clothes.

    A. wear   B. weer   C. ware

6. The _____ was cold in the winter.

    A. are   B. aer   C. air

7. Make a left _____ into the driveway.

    A. tern   B. tirn   C. turn

8. Always play _____.

    A. fair   B. far   C. fiar

9. I bought a _____ of black shoes.

    A. pare   B. pair   C. parr

10. A mother will _____ for her child.

    A. cair   B. chair   C. care

11. You can get a _____ if you get too close to the fire.

    A. burn   B. burne   C. bern

12. I wanted to go _____.

    A. thare   B. theer   C. there

13. Do not _____ at the sun.

    A. stair   B. stare   C. staer

14. If you run too fast, you might get _____.

    A. hirt   B. hert   C. hurt

15. Do not get in a _____ when you take a test.

    A. hurry   B. hurre   C. hirry

Unit 18
Review of lessons 13-17
Part 4

Circle the letter of the correct spelling for the word that belongs in the blank.

1. I _____ a zebra at the zoo.

    A. sow   B. sau   C. saw

2. I like to study _____.

    A. law   B. lau   C. low

3. There was a polar _____ in the water.

    A. bair   B. bear   C. bare

4. A _____ is a big bird.

    A. hawk   B. hauk   C. hake

5. _____ did David hide?

    A. Wear   B. Where   C. Ware

6. A baby deer is called a _____.

    A. fane   B. faun   C. fawn

7. The _____ tasted so good.

    A. slau   B. slaw   C. slaue

8. A bad tooth can make your _____ hurt.

    A. jaw   B. jau   C. gaw

9. Drink from a _____.

    A. strawe   B. strau   C. straw

10. _____ van was blue.

    A. There   B. Their   C. They

11. If you are sleepy, you might _____.

    A. yaun   B. yane   C. yawn

12. I wish Mike would mow the _____.

    A. lown   B. lawn   C. lawne

13. Can you _____ a dinosaur?

    A. draw   B. drow   C. drew

14. I like to eat _____ cabbage.

    A. raw   B. row   C. rau

15. Lay out the frozen meat to let it _____.

    A. thou   B. thaw   C. thau

Unit 24
Review of lessons 19-23
Part 1

Circle the letter of the correct spelling for the word that belongs in the blank.

1. Goliath was a _____ .

    A. gient   B. jint   C. giant

2. I saw a tiger at the _____ .

    A. cercus   B. circus   C. curcus

3. It had been in a _____ .

    A. cage   B. kaje   C. kage

4. I did not want to touch its _____ .

    A. chin   B. gin   C. chen

5. It costs more than a _____ to go to the circus.

    A. sent   B. cent   C. cint

6. I do not want another _____ to go to it.

    A. chence   B. chanse   C. chance

7. I think there is too much _____ to be there.

    A. dangur   B. denjer   C. danger

233

8. I was scared _____ I was there.

    A. while   B. whele   C. whil

9. The animals were _____.

    A. larg   B. large   C. lurge

10. The tigers were _____ and black.

    A. orang   B. orange   C. orenge

11. I am for _____ I do not want to go back.

    A. sertain   B. certian   C. certain

12. The circus was in a big _____.

    A. city   B. citie   C. sity

13. I don't think you will _____ my mind.

    A. chenge   B. change   C. chanje

14. The elephants can walk in a _____.

    A. circel   B. sirkle   C. circle

15. Spin the _____ to play the game.

    A. weel   B. wheel   C. whil

Unit 24
Review of lessons 19-23
Part 2

Circle the letter of the correct spelling for the word that belongs in the blank.

1. _____ Diana was very pretty in her wedding dress.

   A. Prinsess   B. Princess   C. Prencess

2. _____ did John call me?

   A. Why   B. Whi   C. Whye

3. I did not _____ the dog.

   A. catch   B. cach   C. catsh

4. You should not _____ to be sick.

   A. pretind   B. pretend   C. pertend

5. I want to _____ people to read.

   A. teech   B. taech   C. teach

6. The _____ was a toddler.

   A. cheld   B. child   C. childe

7. We bought a toy plane for his birthday _____.

   A. presint   B. persent   C. present

8. I wanted James to _____ quietly.

    A. whisper   B. wisper   C. whispre

9. You can measure one _____ with a ruler.

    A. ench   B. inch   C. insh

10. The green dress was very _____.

    A. prette   B. pritty   C. pretty

11. I got a new _____.

    A. wotch   B. watch   C. wotsh

12. Lillie liked for me to _____ her.

    A. chase   B. chaes   C. chasie

13. I was _____ to have won the contest.

    A. prowd   B. prode   C. proud

14. The _____ was two candy bars.

    A. priez   B. prise   C. prize

15. The green snake was on the tree _____.

    A. branch   B. branche   C. brench

Unit 24
Review of lessons 19-23
Part 3

Circle the letter of the correct spelling for the word that belongs in the blank.

1. I wanted to wear the red _____.

    A. dres   B. dresse   C. dress

2. The alarm on the _____ was set.

    A. clock   B. clok   C. cloke

3. The _____ fell into the sink.

    A. glas   B. glass   C. glase

4. Lynn packed the _____ into the trailer.

    A. clothes   B. close   C. clothees

5. Robert was the _____ of the cab.

    A. drivrr   B. drivur   C. driver

6. She had a bad _____.

    A. dreme   B. dream   C. dreem

7. I had one black _____.

    A. glove   B. gluv   C. gluve

8. They painted the piano _____.

    A. blak   B. blake   C. black

9. I like to _____ the van.

    A. driv   B. drive   C. driev

10. I put _____ on the pictures.

    A. gleu   B. glue   C. gluee

11. Foxes are supposed to be _____.

    A. clever   B. clevr   C. klever

12. She _____ the van into town.

    A. dover   B. drov   C. drove

13. Donna liked to _____ the tree.

    A. clime   B. clim   C. climb

14. Jimmy likes to _____ lemonade.

    A. drink   B. drenk   C. drinke

15. I am _____ we have our own camper.

    A. glade   B. glad   C. gled

Unit 24
Review of lessons 19-23
Part 4

Circle the letter of the correct spelling for the word that belongs in the blank.

1. I made a _____ for Byron.

    A. blankit   B. blanket   C. blenkit

2. A circle is _____.

    A. rownd   B. rond   C. round

3. I put a _____ on the envelope.

    A. stampe   B. stomp   C. stamp

4. I got the _____ of wood.

    A. block   B. blok   C. bloc

5. Go _____ the auto parts store and turn left.

    A. past   B. paste   C. pest

6. The water _____ was not working.

    A. pup   B. pump   C. pumpe

7. Please _____ the door before we go to bed.

    A. loke   B. lok   C. lock

8. You may _____ the balloon up for me.

    A. blow   B. blo   C. blou

9. Do not _____ over the fire.

    A. jumpe   B. jump   C. jamp

10. I made a _____ of things to do.

    A. list   B. lest   C. liste

11. I was _____ asleep.

    A. allmost   B. awmost   C. almost

12. You may _____ when the bride walks down the aisle.

    A. stend   B. stand   C. stund

13. Ben was in the hospital because he was _____.

    A. sick   B. sic   C. sik

14. If felt like I had a _____ in my throat.

    A. lumpe   B. lup   C. lump

15. The money was not _____.

    A. loste   B. lost   C. lots

Unit 30
Review lessons 25-29
Part 1

Circle the letter of the correct spelling of the word.

1. The _____ fur was brown.

    A. rabbit's   B. rabbits'   C. rabit's

2. The _____ muffler was loud.

    A. truk's   B. trucks'   C. truck's

3. Our _____ piano is red, white, and blue.

    A. school's   B. skool's   C. schol's

4. A rock is _____ than a pillow.

    A. herder   B. harder   C. hardar

5. The _____ bike was black.

    A. boys   B. boi's   C. boy's

6. My _____ other car was blue.

    A. moms   B. mom's   C. mam's

7. Drink the _____ water.

    A. frasher   B. fresher   C. freshur

8. The little _____ hair was curly.

    A. girls'   B. gril's   C. girl's

9. The _____ fishing pole was long.

    A. dad's   B. daad's   C. dab's

10. The _____ legs were very short.

    A. doogs   B. dogg's   C. dog's

11. The _____ singing was great.

    A. man's   B. maan's   C. mans

12. James is sometimes _____ than Lynn.

    A. kindeer   B. kinder   C. kiender

13. My _____ car was red.

    A. freind's   B. friend's   C. friende's

14. The _____ cry was pitiful.

    A. child's   B. chield's   C. chid's

15. The _____ voice was soft.

    A. ladie's   B. ladys   C. lady's

Unit 30
Review lessons 25-29
Part 2

Circle the letter of the correct spelling of the word.

1. I would like to be the _____ person in town.

    A. kiendest	B. kindst	C. kindest

2. I _____ on the top step.

    A. steped	B. stepped	C. steeped

3. Cookies are _____ than meat.

    A. sweeter	B. sweater	C. sweetar

4. Some bananas are _____ than others.

    A. greaner	B. greener	C. grener

5. That ear of corn is not the _____.

    A. freshest	B. fresest	C. feshest

6. Lilly should have been _____ down.

    A. siteng	B. siting	C. sitting

7. The _____ bananas will say ripe longer.

    A. grenest	B. greenest	C. greanest

8. We were _____ David stay with us.

    A. letting   B. leting   C. litting

9. Isaiah ran _____ than Vickie did.

    A. fastur   B. fester   C. faster

10. The truck _____ in the snow.

    A. stopped   B. stoped   C. stooped

11. The people _____ their hands.

    A. claped   B. clapeed   C. clapped

12. Were you _____ upset?

    A. geting   B. getting   C. gitting

13. Which candy is the _____?

    A. sweetist   B. sweetest   C. swetest

14. Some people say English is the _____ language to learn.

    A. hardest   B. hardiest   C. hardist

15. Who was the _____ runner in the class?

    A. fastist   B. fasttest   C. fastest

Unit 30
Review lessons 25-29
Part 3

Circle the letter of the correct spelling of the word.

1. Children should not play with _____.

   A. maches   B. matchs   C. matches

2. The baby _____ when he looked at me.

   A. grinned   B. grined   C. grinnd

3. One foot is twelve _____.

   A. inches   B. enches   C. inchs

4. We _____ popcorn in the microwave.

   A. poped   B. popped   C. poppd

5. Do _____ live in the zoo?

   A. fockes   B. foxs   C. foxes

6. I packed several _____ for our vacation.

   A. dreses   B. dresss   C. dresses

7. We needed _____ to pack my dad's dishes.

   A. boxes   B. bockes   C. boxs

8. The sleepy baby _____ his eyes.

    A. rubed   B. rubbed   C. rubbd

9. How many _____ were going to the park?

    A. classes   B. clases   C. classs

10. The girls _____ on one foot.

    A. hoped   B. hoppd   C. hopped

11. Psalm 37:25 says, "I have not seen the righteous forsaken, nor his seed _____ bread."

    A. beging   B. begging   C. beggeng

12. Lynn _____ she had a deck on the front of her house.

    A. wishes   B. weshes   C. wishis

13. Vickie _____ the road closely.

    A. wutches   B. wotches   C. watches

14. James wanted to get new _____.

    A. glesses   B. glases   C. glasses

15. The fish could have _____ into the water.

    A. flupped   B. flopped   c. floped

Unit 30
Review lessons 25-29
Part 4

Circle the letter of the correct spelling of the word.

1. I washed the _____ before we left.

   A. dishis   B. dishes   C. deshes

2. My leg was hurt _____.

   A. badly   B. badle   C. bedly

3. Donna spoke _____.

   A. soffly   B. softly   C. softtly

4. The choir sang _____.

   A. loudly   B. louddly   C. loudlee

5. There is a _____ adult camp meeting at Shady Springs.

   A. yerly   B. yeerly   C. yearly

6. Vickie _____ walked past her dad's casket.

   A. sadlee   B. sadly   C. sedly

7. It is _____ time to start the meeting.

   A. neerly   B. neerlee   C. nearly

8. Cassia _____ walked down the aisle.

   A. sloly	B. slowly	C. slouly

9. David _____ threw a stone at Goliath.

   A. bravly	B. braveely	C. bravely

10. There were two _____ in one package.

    A. brushes	B. brushs	C. brashes

11. Kris felt _____ .

    A. lonely	B. lonly	C. loanly

12. I have _____ young children enrolled in my class.

    A. mostlee	B. mostly	C. mosttly

13. Many _____ broke from the trees.

    A. brunches	B. branchs	C. branches

14. It is hard to see _____ while driving in thick fog.

    A. cleerly	B. clealy	C. clearly

15. I _____ believe vitamin C will help to keep you from catching a cold.

    A. partly	B. parrtly	C. pertly

Unit 36
Review lessons 31-35
Part 1

Circle the letter of the correct spelling of the word.

1. Do not go _____ in the rain.

    A. owt   B. awt   C. out

2. Do you live in a big _____?

    A. toon   B. town   C. toun

3. The men put shingles on the _____.

    A. rouf   B. roof   C. rooph

4. _____ is the man that is speaking.

    A. Who   B. Hwo   C. Whoo

5. I hope Sarah can _____ money.

    A. cout   B. cownt   C. count

6. The people wanted to build a _____.

    A. tower   B. touer   C. towre

7. We heard an _____ hoot outside our home.

    A. oul   B. owl   C. owle

8. My _____ is blue.

    A. house   B. howse   C. hous

9. Did you hear a wolf _____?

    A. howle   B. howl   C. houl

10. Mara pulled her _____.

    A. tuth   B. tooth   C. touth

11. Will Sally talk _____ enough for us to hear?

    A. loud   B. lowd   C. lood

12. Kevin wanted to give Jasmine a pink _____.

    A. flowre   B. flouer   C. flower

13. The _____ of a tornado is like a train.

    A. sownd   B. soud   C. sound

14. _____ far do you live from school?

    A. Whou   B. How   C. Hou

15. The _____ got caught in the trap.

    A. mowse   B. moose   C. mouse

Unit 36
Review lessons 31-35
Part 2

Circle the letter of the correct spelling of the word.

1. I had one blue _____.

   A. baloon   B. balloon   C. bloon

2. I _____ a man named Richard.

   A. knew   B. new   C. knoo

3. A _____ might ride a horse.

   A. cowgirl   B. cougirl   C. cowgril

4. Frankie got a _____.

   A. harecut   B. haircute   C. haircut

5. The balloons were _____.

   A. bloo   B. bluoe   C. blue

6. I like to drink orange _____.

   A. joose   B. juice   C. juise

7. Park the car in the _____.

   A. carport   B. corport   C. carpart

8. He put the milk in the _____.

    A. isebox   B. iceboxe   C. icebox

9. A hammer is a _____.

    A. tewl   B. tool   C. toole

10. Sweep the porch with a _____.

    A. brom   B. brewm   C. broom

11. Did _____ see the wreck?

    A. anyone   B. aneone   C. anywon

12. I could see a _____ of the tree.

    A. roote   B. root   C. rewt

13. Which _____ did Eve eat?

    A. froot   B. fruit   C. frewt

14. Did you see the _____?

    A. sailboat   B. saleboat   C. sail bote

15. The helium balloons _____ high in the sky.

    A. floo   B. flue   C. flew

Unit 36
Review lessons 31-35
Part 3

Circle the letter of the correct spelling of the word.

1. Do not put your finger into your _____.

    A. eye   B. eie   C. eyy

2. Do not stay up past your _____.

    A. bedtim   B. bedtime   C. bedtiem

3. We went to see the Cumberland _____.

    A. waterfaul   B. woterfall   C. waterfall

4. The man walked _____ us.

    A. buy   B. by   C. bie

5. _____ am expensive machine.

    A. Ites   B. Its   C. It's

6. _____ was quiet at the meeting.

    A. Evereone   B. Everyone   C. Everywon

7. The meeting lasted more than one _____.

    A. hour   B. our   C. howr

8. We were not using a _____ on the table.

    A. tabelcloth   B. tableclothe   C. tablecloth

9. _____ was the winner.

    A. Eye   B. I   C. Ie

10. James wanted to _____ some bread.

    A. bye   B. by   C. buy

11. A bird was flying _____ the store.

    A. inside   B. enside   C. insid

12. _____ van is white.

    A. Are   B. Our   C. Oru

13. The Delta Queen _____ the race.

    A. won   B. one   C. wun

14. We stood by the _____ to get warm.

    A. fierside   B. fiersid   C. fireside

15. Some dogs have a bark that sound bigger than _____ bite.

    A. its   B it's   C. ets

Unit 36
Review lessons 31-35
Part 4

Circle the letter of the correct spelling of the word.

1. _____ go to town with me?

    A. ho'll   B. who'll   C. who'ill

2. _____ Mara want candy?

    A. dedn't   B. diden't   C. didn't

3. Vickie _____ ever had a speeding ticket.

    A. hasn't   B. hasen't   C. hesn't

4. Mike bought more than _____ piano.

    A. won   B. once   C. one

5. I _____ buy all the wooden chairs.

    A. won't   B. willn't   C. woen't

6. _____ been learning about turtles.

    A. You've   B. yuov'e   C. youh've

7. _____ been learning the countries of Africa.

    A. Wea've   B. We've   C. Weh've

8. _____ we do if it snows today?

    A. Wat'll   B. What'ill   C. What'll

9. _____ we wear boots when walking in snow?

    A. shooldn't   B. shouldn't   C. shuoldn't

10. Summer isn't _____ yet.

    A. hear   B. here   C. heer

11. I _____ eaten any peach cobbler.

    A. haden't   B. hodn't   C. hadn't

12. _____ be cold if you don't dress warmly at the North Pole.

    A. Yu'll   B. You'll   C. Youw'll

13. I _____ lift a car by myself.

    A. couldn't   B. culdn't   C. cooldn't

14. I like to _____ good music.

    A. here   B. heer   C. hear

15. It _____ nice to be selfish.

    A. isn't   B. esn't   C. isen't

Answer Key

Unit 1

Page 4

A. 1. camp 2. crash
    3. apple 4. dragon
    5. ranch 6. flash

B. 1. penny 2. clever
    3. check 4. spend
    5. bless 6. blend

C. 1. penny 2. clever
    3. apple 4. dragon

D. 1. crash 2. ranch
    3. flash

E. check

Page 5

A. 1. apple 2. penny 3. bless 4. crash 5. ranch 6. clever

B. 1. blend 2. camp   3. check 4. dragon 5. flash 6. spend

Page 6

1. dragon   2. ranch   3. camp   4. Blend
5. penny   6. clever   7. crash   8. check
9. spend   10. Bless   11. flash 12. apple

Unit 2

Page 10

A. 1. shock   2. rock   B. 1. still   2. grill
   3. pond   4. glob   3. splint   4. glimmer

C. 1. cluster   2. flush   D. 1. cluster   2. glimmer
   3. crush   4. brunch

E. 1. still   2. grill   F. 1. flush   2. crush
   3. glimmer   3. brunch

Page 11

A. 1. shock   2. pond   3. glob   4. brunch   5. grill   6. splint

B. 1. cluster   2. crush   3. flush   4. glimmer   5. rock   6. still

Page 12

1. grill   2. brunch   3. rock   pond   4. cluster
5. crush   splint   6. flush   7. shock   8. glimmer
9. glob   10. still

Unit 3

Page 16

A. 1. land 2. sang B. 1. drink 2. twin
   3. drop 4. truck   3. silver 4. until

C. 1. when 2. fence D. 1. truck 2. until

E. 1. began 2. silver 3. dollar 4. until

Page 17
1. fence	2. when	3. silver	4. drop
5. dollar	6. land	7. sang	8. truck
9. twin	10. began	11. drink	12. until

Page 18
1. began	2. land	3. sang	4. fence
5. until	6. drink	7. truck	8. silver
9. When	10. twin	11. drop	12. dollar

Unit 4

Page 22
A. 1. head   2. read   3. ahead   4. lead   5. thread   6. instead
B. 1. ready   2. ahead   3. breakfast   4. heavy   5. instead   6. weather
C. already
D. 1. already   2. ready   3. heavy
E. 1. headed   2. heading

Page 23
1. already   2. weather   3. breath   4. breakfast
5. heavy   6. thread   7. ready   8. instead
9. ahead   10. lead   11. read   12. head

Page 24
1. breakfast   2. already   3. instead   4. ready
5. ahead   6. heavy   7. lead   8. weather
9. head   10. read   11. thread   12. breath

Unit 5

Page 28

A. 1. good   2. stood   B. 1. hum   2. under
    3. wooden   4. pull   3. uncle   4. butter
    5. bush   6. could   5. supper   6. husband

C. 1. wooden   2. under   3. uncle
    4. butter   5. supper   6. husband

Page 29

A. 1. bush   2. could   3. good
    4. hum   5. pull   6. stood

B. 1. wood-en   2. un-der   3. un-cle
    4. but-ter   5. sup-per   6. hus-band

C. 1. uncle   2. supper   3. stood   4. husband

Page 30

1. husband   2. good   3. uncle   4. supper
5. hum   6. wooden   7. butter   8. under
9. could   10. pull   11. stood   12. bush

Spelling Review 6
(answers)

Part 1	Part 2	Part 3	Part 4
1. C	1. A	1. B	1. C
2. B	2. B	2. C	2. A
3. B	3. A	3. A	3. B
4. C	4. C	4. B	4. C
5. A	5. B	5. C	5. A
6. A	6. C	6. A	6. B
7. B	7. B	7. C	7. B
8. A	8. C	8. C	8. C
9. B	9. A	9. B	9. A
10. C	10. A	10. A	10. C
11. B	11. C	11. B	11. B
12. A	12. B	12. B	12. C
13. C	13. B	13. C	13. B
14. C	14. C	14. A	14. A
15. A	15. C	15. A	15. A

Unit 7

Page 35

A. 1. shave 2. state
3. plate 4. flame

B. 1. wise 2. glide
3. white 4. smile

C. 1. stole 2. close
3. broke 4. stove

D. 1. state 2. stole
3. stove

E. 1. shave 2. white

Page 36

A. 1. shave 2. wise 3. plate
4. broke 5. flame 6. white
7. stove 8. stole

B. 1. close 2. glide 3. smile 4. state

C. 1. smile 2. close

Page 37

A. 1. broke 2. state 3. smile 4. white
5. wise 6. stove 7. glide 8. flame
9. stole 10. shave 11. close 12. plate

Unit 8

Page 41

A. 1. rain 2. paid B. 1. stay 2. today
3. wait 4. afraid 3. away 4. maybe
5. paint 6. plain 5. hay 6. tray

C. 1. afraid 2. today D. 1. maybe 2. today
3. away 4. maybe

Page 42

A. 1. maybe 2. afraid 3. rain
4. paid 5. wait 6. today

B. 1. away 2. hay 3. paint
4. plain 5. stay 6. tray

C. 1. rain 2. afraid 3. Maybe

Page 43

1. paint 2. paid 3. away 4. rain
5. hay 6. tray 7. afraid 8. wait
9. plain 10. today 11. Maybe 12. stay

Unit 9

Page 47

A. 1. road 2. coat
   3. load 4. boat

B. 1. hold 2. fold

C. 1. ago 2. over
   3. open 4. only
   5. hello

D. 1. hello

E. toe

Page 48

A. 1. fold 2. only open over
   3. boat 4. toe

B. 1. boat 2. coat 3. hello
   4. hold 5. load 6. road

Page 49

A. 1. hold 2. ago 3. boat 4. over
   5. only 6. open 7. road 8. hello
   9. fold 10. coat 11. toe 12. load

  B. 1. fold 2. coat

Unit 10

Page 53

A. 1. seat   2. clean
    3. read   4. mean
    5. leap

B. 1. peep   2. feel
    3. asleep 4. street
    5. peek   6. keep
    7. needle

C. 1. asleep   2. needle

D. 1. peek   2. feel

Page 54

A. 1. clean   2. peep
    3. seat   4. leap

B. 1. asleep 2. feel   3. mean
    4. peek   5. read   6. street

C. 1. clean   2. mean   3. asleep   4. keep

Page 55

1. needle   2. keep   3. asleep   4. seat
5. peep   6. clean   7. street   8. peek
9. read   10. feel   11. mean   12. leap

Unit 11

Page 59

A. 1. my 2. cry 3. dry 4. sky 5. fly

B. 1. high 2. light 3. night 4. right 5. bright

C. 1. tie 2. lie

D. 1. high 2. light

Page 60

A. 1. high 2. light 3. right 4. dry 5. night 6. cry 7. sky 8. tie

B. 1. bright 2. lie 3. my 4. fly

C. Answers may vary.

Page 61

A. 1. fly 2. high 3. sky 4. tie right 5. night 6. bright 7. dry 8. cry 9. lie 10. light 11. My

Spelling Review 12
(answers)

Part 1	Part 2	Part 3	Part 4
1. C	1. A	1. B	1. B
2. B	2. C	2. A	2. A
3. C	3. C	3. A	3. C
4. A	4. B	4. C	4. A
5. A	5. A	5. A	5. C
6. B	6. B	6. C	6. B
7. C	7. C	7. B	7. B
8. B	8. A	8. A	8. A
9. A	9. A	9. C	9. C
10. C	10. B	10. C	10. A
11. A	11. B	11. B	11. C
12. B	12. C	12. A	12. B
13. A	13. B	13. B	13. B
14. C	14. A	14. A	14. C
15. B	15. C	15. C	15. A

Unit 13

Page 66

A. 1. short   2. born   B. 1. store   2. more
    3. horse   4. fork   3. score
    5. north   6. story

C. 1. roar   2. board

D. pour

Page 67

A. 1. f   2. e   3. a
    4. b   5. d   6. c

B. 1. more   2. short
    3. north   4. born

C. 1. store   2. fork   3. horse

Page 68

1. roar   2. score   3. pour   4. north
5. horse   6. more   7. store   8. born
9. board   10. short   11. story   12. fork

Unit 14

Page 72

A. 1. worm 2. work B. 1. person 2. were
3. word 4. worth
5. worry

C. 1. earn 2. early 3. earth

D. 1. worry 2. early 3. person

Page 73

A. 1. work 2. earth 3. word 4. heard 5. were
6. learn 7. earn 8. worth 9. worm 10. worry

B. 1. worm 2. were 3. learn
4. word 5. earth 6. worry

C. 1. worm 2. earth

Page 74

1. work 2. worm 3. learn 4. person
5. early 6. word 7. were 8. worry
9. heard 10. worth 11. earth 12. earn

Unit 15

Page 78

A. 1. bird   2. shirt   B. 1. turn   2. burn
    3. first   4. third   3. hurt   4. church
    5. sir   6. birthday   5. turtle   6. hurry

C. 1. birthday   2. turtle   3. hurry

D. 1. bird   2. turtle

Page 79

A. 1. bird   2. shirt   3. first   4. sir   5. third
    6. hurt   7. burn   8. turn   9. hurry   10. church

B. 1. first   2. bird   birthday   3. turn   turtle
    4. hurry   hurt   5. shirt   sir   6. third
    7. church   8. burn

Page 80

1. first   2. turn   3. burn   4. church
5. bird   6. sir   7. hurry   8. shirt
9. third   10. birthday   11. hurt   12. turtle

Unit 16

Page 84

A. 1. air   2. fair   B. 1. care   2. stare
    3. stairs   4. pair
    5. chair

C. there

D. 1. wear   2. where

Page 85

A. 1. fair   2. stares   3. there   4. pair   5. bear

B. 1) wear   2) there   their   3) stairs   stare
    4) care   5) where   6) air
    7) chair   8) bear   care

Page 86

A. 1. airline   2. careless   3. anywhere   4. upstairs

B. 1. air   air   2. wear   wear

C. 1. pair   2. Fair   3. there   4. chair   5. bear   stare

Unit 17

Page 90

A. 1. raw 2. jaw
3. straw 4. thaw
5. saw 6. draw
7. slaw 8. draw

B. 1. lawn 2. yawn
3. fawn 4. hawk

C. jaw

D. 1. fawn 2. hawk

Page 91

A. 1. jaw 2. saw 3. draw 4. slaw 5. yawn 6. straw

B. 1. raw 2. law 3. thaw
4. lawn 5. fawn 6. hawk

C. 1. saw 2. saw

Page 92

A. 1. straw 2. yawn 3. raw 4. hawk
5. thaw 6. law 7. fawn 8. slaw
9. draw 10. jaw 11. lawn 12. saw

273

Spelling Review 18
(answers)

Part 1	Part 2	Part 3	Part 4
1. C	1. A	1. B	1. C
2. A	2. C	2. B	2. A
3. B	3. A	3. C	3. B
4. B	4. B	4. A	4. A
5. A	5. B	5. A	5. B
6. C	6. C	6. C	6. C
7. B	7. A	7. C	7. B
8. A	8. C	8. A	8. A
9. C	9. B	9. B	9. C
10. C	10. B	10. C	10. B
11. B	11. C	11. A	11. C
12. C	12. B	12. C	12. B
13. A	13. A	13. B	13. A
14. A	14. A	14. C	14. A
15. B	15. C	15. A	15. B

Unit 19

Page 97

A. 1. cent 2. circle
    3. certain 4. circus
    5. chance 6. city

B. 1. giant 2. cage
    3. large 4. orange
    5. change 6. danger

C. cent

D. 1. change 2. cent 3. large 4. chance

Page 98

A. 1. cir-cle 2. cer-tain 3. cir-cus
   4. gi-ant 5. o-range 6. dan-ger
   7. cit-y

B. 1. circle 2. chance 3. change
   4. cage 5. large 6. cent

C. 1. certain 2. orange

Page 99

A. 1. circus 2. danger 3. orange 4. large
   5. cage 6. certain 7. city 8. cent chance
   9. change 10. giant 11. circles

Unit 20

Page 103

A. 1. chin   2. chase   B. 1. watch   2. catch
    3. child

C. 1. branch   2. teach   3. inch

D. 1. wheel   2. while   3. why   4. whisper

Page 104

A. 1. (3)   2. (1)   3. (2)
    4. (3)   5. (1)   6. (1)

B. 1. chin   2. watch   3. teach   4. catch   5. wheel
    6. branch   7. inch   8. chase   9. whisper

Page 105

1. while   2. catch   3. teach   4. whisper
5. chase   6. watch   7. inch   8. wheel
9. chin   10. branch   11. child   12. Why

Unit 21

Page 109

A. 1. prize 2. proud
   3. princess 4. present
   5. pretend 6. pretty

B. 1. drive 2. drove
   3. dress 4. drink
   5. dream 6. driver

C. 1. prize 2. drive 3. driver

D. 1. driver

Page 110

A. 1. prize 2. drink 3. dress
   4. drive 5. drove 6. dream
   7. princess 8. present

B. 1. prin-cess 2. driv-er 3. pres-ent 4. pret-ty 5. pre-tend

C. 1. proud 2. pretend 3. dream

Page 111

1. pretend 2. drove 3. prize 4. Princess
5. dream 6. pretty 7. present 8. dress
9. drink 10. drive 11. driver 12. proud

Unit 22

Page 115

A. 1. glad 2. glass B. 1. climb 2. clothes
3. glue 4. glove 3. clock 4. clever

C. 1. black 2. block D. 1. glad 2. glass
3. blow 4. blanket 3. black 4. blanket

Page 116

A. 1. black 2. blanket 3. block 4. blow
1. clever 2. climb 3. clock 4. clothes
1. glad 2. glass 3. glove 4. glue

B. Answers may vary.

Page 117

1. clock 2. glass 3. climb 4. glue
5. glad 6. blow 7. clever 8. black
9. block 10. clothes 11. blanket 12. glove

Unit 23

Page 121

A. 1. pump 2. lump B. 1. list 2. lost
   3. jump 4. stamp   3. almost 4. past

C. 1. stand 2. round

D. 1. lock 2. sick

E. almost

F. 1. stand 2. stamp

Page 122

A. 1. list 2. lost 3. past 4. pump 5. stamp

B. 1. stand 2. sick 3. round
   4. lump 5. lock 6. jump

C. al-most

D. 1. lost 2. sick

Page 123

1. stand 2. list 3. round 4. lost
5. sick 6. lump 7. lock 8. stamp
9. past 10. almost 11. jump 12. pump

Spelling Review 24
(answers)

Part 1	Part 2	Part 3	Part 4
1. C	1. B	1. C	1. B
2. B	2. A	2. A	2. C
3. A	3. A	3. B	3. C
4. A	4. B	4. A	4. A
5. B	5. C	5. C	5. A
6. C	6. B	6. B	6. B
7. C	7. C	7. A	7. C
8. A	8. A	8. C	8. A
9. B	9. B	9. B	9. B
10. B	10. C	10. B	10. A
11. C	11. B	11. A	11. C
12. A	12. A	12. C	12. B
13. B	13. C	13. C	13. A
14. C	14. C	14. A	14. C
15. B	15. A	15. B	15. B

Unit 25

Page 128

A. 1. girl's 2. friend's   B. 1. dog's   2. rabbit's
   3. boy's 4. mom's
   5. dad's 6. lady's
   7. man's 8. child's

C. truck's

D. rabbit's

E. 1. lady's 2. rabbit's

Page 129

A. 1. friend's   2. school's   3. truck's   4. lady's

B. 1. o   2. mo   3. f n   4. oy   5. a y   6. i

C. 1. rabbit's   2. man's   3. child's   4. dad's

D. 1. boy's   2. man's   3. mom's

Page 130

A. 1. lady's   2. mom's   3. dog's   4. school's
   5. friend's   6. truck's   7. rabbit's

B. 8. man's   9. girl's   10. boy's
   11. child's   12. dad'

Unit 26

Page 134

A. 1. kinder 2. harder   B. 1. kindest 2. hardest
    3. fresher 4. faster   3. freshest 4. fastest
    5. greener 6. sweeter   5. greenest 6. sweetest

C. 1. greener 2. greenest

D. 1. sweeter 2. sweetest

E. 1. fresher 2. freshest

Page 135

A. 1. harder 2. kindest 3. freshest 4. faster

B. 1. hardest 2. kinder 3. fastest 4. freshest

C. 1. greener 2. fresher 3. sweeter
    4. sweetest 5. harder

Page 136

1. faster fastest 2. greener greenest
3. kinder kindest 4. harder hardest
5. fresher freshest 6. sweeter sweetest

282

Unit 27

Page 140

A. 1. grinned   2. stopped
    3. stepped   4. clapped
    5. getting

B. 1. i e   2. o e
    3. e i   4. i i
    5. u e   6. o e
    7. e i   8. o e

C. 1. stopped   2. stepped   3. clapped
    4. grinned   5. flopped

Page 141

A. 1. pop   2. rub   3. let   4. step   5. sit   6. hop

B. 1. grinned   2. clapped   3. rubbed   4. begging

C. 1. popped   2. stopped   3. stepped
    4. hopped   5. grinned

Page 142

1. sitting   2. stepped   3. grinned   4. letting
5. popped   6. clapped   7. flopped   8. getting
9. rubbed   10. hopped   11. begging   12. stopped

283

Unit 28

Page 146

A. 1. foxes 2. boxes B. 1. watches 2. matches
                         3. inches 4. branches

C. 1. glasses 2. dresses 3. classes

D. 1. wishes 2. brushes 3. dishes

Page 147

A. 1. boxes 2. brushes 3. classes 4. wishes
   5. matches 6. foxes 7. glasses 8. branches
   9. dishes 10. inches 11. watches 12. dresses

B. 1. glasses 2. dishes 3. foxes

Page 148

1. brushes 2. inches 3. foxes 4. classes
5. matches 6. glasses 7. branches 8. wishes
9. dresses 10. boxes 11. watches 12. dishes

Unit 29

Page 152

A. 1. loudly   2. softly   3. badly   4. partly
    5. clearly   6. yearly   7. sadly   8. nearly
    9. mostly   10. bravely 11. lonely 12. slowly

B. 1. nearly   2. yearly   3. clearly

C. bravely

D. partly

Page 153

A. 1. mostly   2. nearly   3. bravely
    4. partly   5. slowly   6. softly

B. 1. nearly   2. clearly   3. badly   4. sadly

C. 1. softly   2. yearly   3. lonely   4. loudly

Page 154

1. slowly   2. yearly   3. softly   4. loudly
5. badly   6. bravely   7. sadly   8. clearly
9. partly   10. mostly   11. lonely   12. nearly

Spelling Review 30
(answers)

Part 1	Part 2	Part 3	Part 4
1. A	1. C	1. C	1. B
2. C	2. B	2. A	2. A
3. A	3. A	3. A	3. B
4. B	4. B	4. B	4. A
5. C	5. A	5. C	5. C
6. B	6. C	6. C	6. B
7. B	7. B	7. A	7. C
8. C	8. A	8. B	8. B
9. A	9. C	9. A	9. C
10. C	10. A	10. C	10. A
11. A	11. C	11. B	11. A
12. B	12. B	12. A	12. B
13. B	13. B	13. C	13. C
14. A	14. A	14. C	14. C
15. C	15. C	15. B	15. A

Unit 31

Page 159

A. 1. loud   2. out   B. 1. town   2. tower
    3. house   4. count   3. howl   4. flower
    5. sound   6. mouse   5. owl   6. how

C. 1. tower   2. flower

D. 1. mouse   2. tower   3. howl

Page 160

A. 1. count   2. loud   3. town   4. howl
    5. mouse   6. owl   7. house   8. flower

B. 1. ou   2. ow   3. ow   4. ow

C. 1. count   2. flower   3. mouse   4. sound

Page 161

1. house   2. flower   3. sound   4. loud
5. out   6. How   7. mouse   8. town
9. count   10. howl   11. owl   12. tower

Unit 32

Page 165

A. 1. tooth 2. roof
   3. balloon 4. root
   5. tool 6. broom

B. 1. fruit 2. juice

C. 1. flew 2. knew

D. who

E. blue

Page 166

A. 1. fruit 2. tool 3. juice 4. root 5. who
   6. flew 7. balloon 8. broom 9. knew

B. 1. blue 2. knew

C. 1. roof 2. tooth 3. balloon

Page 167

1. tooth 2. root 3. tool 4. who
5. juice   fruit

6. balloon   roof 7. flew
8. knew 9. blue
10. broom

Unit 33

Page 171

A. 1. everyone   2. anyone   B. 1. fireside   2. inside

C. 1. cowgirl   2. carport

D. 1. everyone   2. anyone   3. tablecloth   4. waterfall

E. 1. haircut   2. sailboat   3. icebox   4. bedtime

Page 172

A. 1. cowgirl   2. bedtime   3. anyone
   4. inside   5. haircut   6. fireside

B. 1. carport   2. icebox   3. sailboat   4. everyone
   5. tablecloth 6. fireside   7. waterfall

Page 173 **<u>DO NOT HAVE TO BE IN THIS ORDER.</u>**

1. icebox   2. anyone   3. carport   4. bedtime
5. cowgirl   6. inside   7. sailboat   8. fireside
9. tablecloth   10. haircut   11. waterfall   12. everyone

Unit 34

Page 177

A. 1. eye   2. it's   B. it's
    3. buy   4. won
    5. hour   6. hear

C. eye

D. 1. buy   2. by   3. I   4. eye

E. one

Page 178

A. 1. buy   2. by   3. eye   4. hear   5. here
   6. hour   7. its   8. one   9. our   10. won

B. 1. it's   2. hour   3. its
   4. buy   5. here   6. ours

C. one   our

Page 179

1. won   2. our   3. It's   4. hear
5. by   6. here   7. one   8. eye
9. hour   10. its   11. I   12. buy

290

Unit 35

Page 183

A. 1. isn't   2. didn't
    3. won't   4. hasn't
    5. hadn't 6. couldn't
    7. shouldn't

B. 1. who'll   2. you'll
    3. what'll

C. 1. we've   2. you've

D. 1. who'll   2. we've   3. what'll   4. won't

Page 184

1. You'll   2. isn't   3. Who'll   4. Shouldn't
5. What'll   6. We've   7. Won't   8. couldn't
9. hadn't   10. You've 11. Didn't   12. hasn't

Spelling Review 36
(answers)

Part 1	Part 2	Part 3	Part 4
1. C	1. B	1. A	1. B
2. B	2. A	2. B	2. C
3. B	3. A	3. C	3. A
4. A	4. C	4. B	4. C
5. C	5. C	5. C	5. A
6. A	6. B	6. B	6. A
7. B	7. A	7. A	7. B
8. A	8. C	8. C	8. C
9. B	9. B	9. B	9. B
10. B	10. C	10. C	10. B
11. A	11. A	11. A	11. C
12. C	12. B	12. B	12. B
13. C	13. B	13. A	13. A
14. B	14. A	14. C	14. C
15. C	15. C	15. A	15. A

www.ingramcontent.com/pod-product-compliance
Lightning Source LLC
Chambersburg PA
CBHW080332170426
43194CB00014B/2540